# SACRED CHAOS

"Jennifer Stavinoha draws from her degrees in theology and motherhood to deliver a retreat that is both spiritually transformative and infinitely relatable. I found myself nodding along and wishing I had read these words sooner. If you want to re-center your prayer life and encounter Christ in the chaos of motherhood, this book is for you. For anyone who has wondered why combining prayer and motherhood can feel so hard, this book is an encouraging road map to desiring prayer, encountering Christ, and rediscovering joy in your spiritual life."

**Kassie Manning**
Cofounder of Every Sacred Sunday

"*Sacred Chaos* by Jennifer Stavinoha is a consoling and relatable read for Catholic moms aching to find balance in their prayer, motherhood, and the everyday demands of life. For those yearning to grow in their relationship with God while managing the chaos of family life, this book is an invaluable resource. Stavinoha gently helps readers approach the spiritual life through accessible yet deeply insightful reflections, seamlessly weaving in scripture and the rich traditions of the Church. Even as a husband and father, the practical wisdom found on these pages was encouraging for my own prayer life as I navigate the sacred messiness of parenthood. This would make a wonderful gift for your wife—just be sure to read it over her shoulder!"

**Joshua Mazrin**
Author of *Led by the Immaculata* and
Founder of The Immaculata Institute

"This book is a balm to a weary mom's soul, offering encouragement to take moments of quiet to reflect on all that motherhood entails. I loved it and am grateful it's out in the world for moms, in every stage, to pray with."

**Katie Prejean McGrady**
Host of *The Katie McGrady Show* on SiriusXM's The Catholic Channel

# SACRED CHAOS

## FINDING JOY AND JESUS IN THE MESSINESS OF MOTHERHOOD

**A RESTORATIVE 3-WEEK RETREAT**

JENNIFER STAVINOHA

Ave Maria Press AVE Notre Dame, Indiana

---



Founded in 1865, Ave Maria Press is a ministry of the United States Province of Holy Cross.

www.avemariapress.com

Paperback: ISBN-13 978-1-64680-395-8

E-book: ISBN-13 978-1-64680-396-5

Cover image © Getty Images.

Cover and text design by Brianna Dombo.

Printed and bound in the United States of America.

*Library of Congress Cataloging-in-Publication Data is available.*

**TO EVERY MOTHER WHO HAS STRUGGLED WITH DAILY PRAYER, INCLUDING MYSELF**

# CONTENTS

# FOREWORD

I used to find acorns by the handful in my washing machine and dryer. What is it that makes a kid bring the outdoors inside? Inquisitive investigation? Wholesome meddling? Delightful hoarding?

I remembered the acorns one morning when they crunched under my feet as I walked the dogs. I stopped to scoop up my own handful and placed them in my pocket for old time's sake. I took a deep breath and noted the changing of the seasons.

Now that they are getting older, my children are not as interested in acorns as they once were. Diaper bags have turned into gym bags; stinky diapers are now stinky socks. The mornings are quieter than they used to be too. Once the folders have been signed and lunches packed, we scuttle to the van dragging backpacks and jackets and hustle off to school. Then I stand in the kitchen alone, working to remember the nights I was up with the baby and the early mornings I was awakened by four heads at the side of the bed asking for oatmeal. If someone would've told me then that one day (sooner than I thought) I'd have mornings to myself, with plenty of time to wipe the cut strawberry tops from the counter and take the dogs on a leisurely walk before tending to the work I love, I would've replied that this kind of teasing should be considered cruel and unusual.

Yet here I am—taking deep breaths, working to remember—with clean countertops and a pocketful of acorns.

As a mother, I spent a pretty significant chunk of a decade with my kids glued to me. For years I bathed with miniature dinosaurs, plastic farm animals, and limbless Barbies floating around me. I once went to the dentist for a root canal, and as I put in my earbuds, I had the disturbing thought that maybe dental work wasn't so bad because I was finally getting some "me time."

I have never given myself to anything more than I have to my motherhood. But I can see now that my motherhood had me in survival mode only.

My self-donation was exhaustive and complete; it was also broken and flawed. There was joy and strife and then more joy. My kids pushed me to my furthest edges and then pulled me right back in again. I spent time dispensing Goldfish crackers. I hung out in a baby pool. I found the perfect princess dresses at resale shops. I sacrificed my body, my time, and my talent and hoped it was enough to grow these little people into truly good humans. I did all of those things dutifully because I'd never wanted anything more. I also did it in a frenzy because it felt utterly impossible to keep up.

One morning, the stars aligned for me to shop at the grocery store by myself. As tunes from my teenage years wafted through the store speakers, I had a realization: I hadn't experimented in the kitchen in a while, something I used to really enjoy. Hmph. That realization came with a complicated mix of longing and guilt, maybe a dash of resentment. As I worked through my shopping list, I silently made another—this list full of other things I used to do. I used to be in a book club. I used to spend money decorating my house. I used to attend a yoga class. I used to take pride in putting together a cute outfit. I used to meet for brunch with my friends. I used to stay up late and watch a show that my husband and I would dissect later. Then, in front of the paper towels in aisle 13, it dawned on me that over the years I had dismissed myself over and over again. Somewhere in the impossible demand to keep up, the needs of my children, my family, and my partner had come before my own so frequently that I had begun to overlook some fundamental human needs: a need to create using the gifts I've been given, for example. And a need to feel seen, understood, and accounted for.

Who was I anymore? For a mom of five, I wasn't even sure.

I know that when life gets to be too much, my daily time with God suffers. My focus dwindles. My discipline disintegrates. I get distracted by my phone instead of recentering with prayer. Before long, I'm disconnected, disoriented, and confused. After thirty years of practicing this faith, you'd think I'd have it figured out, but unfortunately, this pattern pops up in my life quite often. When the pace gets chaotic, I tend to drift away from the truest parts of me, and the only way back is by returning to the good God who made me. I need to reconnect. I need to remember. I need to pray.

Is it really just as simple as prayer?

I gave up a lot back then when the kids were little. Now that they are older, their needs might not occupy every cell of my body and brain, but the physical demands have been replaced with emotional ones. Their victories and defeats, their friend dramas and breakups, their invitations and exclusions affect me deeply. I'm overscheduled and undernourished. I eat my meals on the go and scroll for spiritual direction. I help with homework while browning the meat. I fall into bed only to stay awake until I hear the car pull in. My back is creaky from sitting on bleachers. My voice is hoarse from rooting them on. I fight the balance of respecting the freedom they now deserve and planning their lives so that they don't ruin them. I have no idea if I'm doing a good job, and it feels that only time will tell. In this way, even though I didn't see it coming, my kids have as much of me as they ever did.

Jennifer Stavinoha is a good friend and a true sister in this work of mothering. I'm not sure where she was ten years ago when I needed this book the most. But I'm discovering that, even with my clean counters and full eight hours of sleep, I need God in this stage of motherhood just as much as I did when these teens were toddlers. This is why I am so grateful for her leadership with this book—it will help us mothers stay connected when we feel pulled past our limits.

As a friend, Jennifer is someone who makes difficult places more tenable. As a mother, Jennifer comes alongside us when motherhood feels lonely or thankless to say, "I know, and I've been there." As a disciple, Jennifer calls us back to our deepest identity, always reminding us of our one true name: Beloved. She has the imagination and heart to lead us to a more expansive understanding of who God is—I know because she has helped me learn so many lessons I treasure: that my questions about my faith aren't rebellion; that motherhood doesn't have to be limiting or restrictive; that my prayers are my most important conversations of the day; that there is no place God can't go.

With this book, Jennifer leads us in a renewed discipline of prayer that isn't chirpy or prescriptive. Our children are—all at once—our greatest joys and our greatest stressors, and in *Sacred Chaos* Jennifer speaks to this duality in a way that makes us feel seen and loved and encouraged. This three-week retreat meets us wherever we are in the midst of new responsibilities, evolving challenges, or hectic schedules and cheerleads us toward deeper intimacy with God. Whether we are sprinting forward with full lungs or barely inching along in a crawl, Jennifer's wisdom and accompaniment points us to prayer with manageable instructions and practical advice.

This book is such a gift. You will undoubtedly read it, reread it, and then give it to every mom you know.

Allison Sullivan<br>
Host of the *Sinner Saint Sister* podcast

# INTRODUCTION

It was a strange experience for me, hearing a friend recount her feelings on how challenging it was to pray as a new mother. Not because I thought prayer as a mom should be easy (I knew too well the opposite was true)—but because her words seemed to come out of time and space, from my own heart years before. "It's not that I don't have the time to pray," she lamented. "But when I do pray, I get nothing. I just miss . . . the intimacy."

There is something unique about prayer as a single person, or as a person without children. I have many memories of deep, intimate prayer with the Lord where I could sit and pray for as long as I liked, both scheduled and unscheduled. For example, when I was in grad school, I remember leaving adoration, walking back to my apartment, and feeling the Lord calling me back to the chapel. So I turned around and went back for another hour. How lovely for me then. How incredibly impossible that feels now.

I also remember that most of my prayer as a single woman was concerned with my future: "Lord, where is my future husband?" "Lord, what do you want me to do with my life?" "Lord, lead me in the right direction." Now that I am living my vocation as a wife and a mother, prayer looks very, very different: "God, please don't let me get this stomach bug that the kids have." "Jesus, help me stay calm in this moment." "Please, Lord, just let this child sleep through the night." Prayer has become a whole lot less ethereal and a whole lot more physical. And yet, there is a desire to meet with the Lord, to hear his voice, and to be intimate with him. As my friend lamented, though, it's difficult to hear God's voice when you have a ten-month-old sucking on your leg.

For years, I struggled with prayer as a mother. At first, I needed to use every spare moment to sleep or shower. Then, I needed to make sure my toddler wasn't going to harm herself. When I finally did find time to pray, I discovered that I would rather just scroll on my phone or take a nap. As the years went by, school pickups, after-school activities, and helping kids with their homework seemed to take the place of actual, intentional prayer. It's not that prayer during the day didn't happen—it absolutely did. But it was mostly in the form of crying out to the Lord when I needed help or guidance. And I found that when I actually did sit down to pray, the guilt of having not prayed would always be the subject of my prayer. The intimacy that had been so deeply cultivated years before was inaccessible.

I was experiencing what so many other mothers experience, yet this loss is rarely acknowledged. I don't think I confided my struggles in prayer to hardly anyone because, as someone who was in ministry with degrees in theology, it was embarrassing. Prayer is the most basic way to be in communion with the Lord, and I couldn't even experience it in any way that was meaningful. The shame was overwhelming, so it was hidden.

This is the reality in motherhood: The exhaustion, both mental and physical, can drain any desire for prayer out of our bodies. Yet, God knew what he was doing when he made motherhood. He knew we would be exhausted. He knew we would be stretched to our limits. He knew our bodies would be wired to keep these humans alive and, hopefully, help them thrive. Did he intend for mothers to simply "take a break" on intimacy with him until our kids grow up? Is prayer only for single people and those who are retired? Absolutely not! I do believe that we are invited to seek him and find him even when our desire runs low and our guilt runs high.

Jesus tells us:

> Ask and it will be given to you; seek and you will find; knock and the door will be opened to you. For everyone

> who asks, receives; and the one who seeks, finds; and to the one who knocks, the door will be opened. Which one of you would hand his son a stone when he asks for a loaf of bread, or a snake when he asks for a fish? If you then, who are wicked, know how to give good gifts to your children, how much more will your heavenly Father give good things to those who ask him. (Mt 7:7–11)

I truly believe that the Lord wants us to desire him above every good in our life. His presence is the highest good we can ever ask for, and he will give it to us when we ask. Every. Time. Maybe we won't feel the tingly, happy feelings that once nourished us. If you do receive consolation, great—you've just received a gift from the Lord. But if not, know that the Lord is still present to you—even in the desert. Even when you don't want to pray and show up anyway. Even if it's been a few days, or months (or years, even?), since you've opened a bible. He does not withhold himself from those who feel distant from him. He is the Father who runs with delight to his child, no matter how long it's been.

In speaking with other moms who are seeking holiness for themselves and their families, I often hear a desire to go deeper with the Lord. We want to be real with him on a level that matches the reality of our lives. Many devotionals, while easy to pick up and read anytime, leave us wanting more than a sweet story and a prayer. "I don't want to read a prayer that someone has prayed for me," one mom lamented. "I want to be set up to speak to the Lord myself." I hope this book will help you do just that.

The first seven days of this book will be all about desire, or lack thereof. As we journey through these days, be honest with God about your desire for him, or the lack of desire you feel. He already knows how you feel, but often we need to say it ourselves in order to move forward. The next seven days, we will journey through the theme of encounter. The Lord is present to us in every moment, whether we feel it or not, but recognizing him when he moves in our lives is another story. The final seven days are all about joy. Joy and happiness are often confused, but they are not the same. Happiness is dependent on our outward circumstances, such as if our kid scores a goal, gets an A on a test, or takes those first steps. Joy, however, is completely dependent on our reliance on the Lord.

My prayer is that you experience intimacy with the Lord through this book. As we begin, I invite you to turn your heart over to the Lord: Be honest with him, and let him transform you from the inside out. He's already here, waiting for us.

# WEEK 1: DESIRE

We begin our journey to the Lord by seeking something that is out of our control to obtain. The desire to enter into prayer is not something we can will ourselves to experience. Many times in life, we will feel ourselves hungering and thirsting for God. During those times, entering into prayer will feel like taking a fresh drink of water. The happy feelings come, and we are rewarded by a sense of fulfillment on a physical and spiritual level.

If you are in this place of consolation right now, that's wonderful. Lean into it. Receive this gift from the Lord, and drink deeply. But if you find prayer difficult—whether from lack of desire or willpower, from guilt, or from disordered priorities—that's okay too. It's here that we start: asking the Lord for the desire to encounter him.

There is a false dichotomy that haunts the Christian world: You can lean into either the intellectual side of the faith or the emotional side—you can't choose both. The intellectual side, some will say, is devoid of relationship. It is dry, purely theoretical, and has no real encounter with the living God. On the other hand are those who allow their emotions to be the entirety of their faith. When their emotions leave, so does their faith. Their experience of God is as if he is not almighty and constant, but sways with the wind and disappears at the first hint of crisis.

Surely, there are pitfalls to staking a claim on either "side" of Catholic spirituality. But God is the God of reason *and* emotion. He wants us to know he is present, he can truly be felt and sensed with our emotions, and he is a strong tower for when our senses fail us. If you feel any sort of emotion in prayer, that's wonderful! But if not, know that the Lord still wants you to desire him and to know him—even if that means you must choose to intentionally show up in prayer rather than wait for your emotions to carry you there.

When I was a campus minister at a Catholic high school, I taught the leadership team how to share a testimony. Each student would write a story about how they had experienced God and share it with the rest of the group. After practicing with the group, they would have the opportunity to share with the rest of the school throughout the year. Listening to each student share how they had personally been impacted by the Lord was such a beautiful experience. There was one girl who was particularly anxious about her talk. After our leadership team meeting one afternoon, she approached me and said, "I can't do this. I don't have a 'big moment' of encountering God like everyone else." "Well," I said, "how do you know that God is real?" Thinking about it for a moment, she replied, "I guess I don't know how I know. I just . . . choose to believe, even though I don't know for sure."

That was it right there. She had not had any emotional aha moment with the Lord, and yet she chose to give her life to Christ anyway. She chose God and his will in her life, even though she couldn't articulate how she knew him to be real. Her testimony is not the kind of remarkable story that earns us an interview at EWTN or a book deal, but it is real. And it is so, *so* needed. Her testimony ended up being the most powerful of all the stories we shared that year because almost every student at that high school could relate to the frustration of not "feeling" God's presence. It helped them to hear from someone who was choosing God anyway.

This week, as we explore desire, we will be positioning our hearts to face the Lord. We will be choosing to seek the Lord, even when we don't feel like it or when we experience dryness in prayer.

## TAKE TO PRAYER

- Take a minute to tell the Lord what you are seeking as we begin this retreat.
- Leave space for the Lord to tell you what he wants from you over this next week.

## WATCH AND LISTEN

To watch a video introduction to this week, scan the QR code or visit www.avemariapress.com/pages/sacred-chaos-resources. You'll also find there a playlist with music to accompany your daily prayer.

## DAY 1

# I WANT TO WANT THIS

---

### IF YOU ONLY HAVE TWO MINUTES TO PRAY TODAY, PRAY THIS:

Jesus, let me desire you today. Deepen my longing for you. Help me want you. And when my emotions don't carry my heart, help my heart to choose you anyway. Amen.

---

## RECEIVE FROM THE WORD

LORD, hear my prayer;
  in your faithfulness listen to my pleading;
  answer me in your righteousness.
Do not enter into judgment with your servant;
  before you no one can be just.
The enemy has pursued my soul;
  he has crushed my life to the ground.
He has made me dwell in darkness
  like those long dead.

My spirit is faint within me;
 my heart despairs.
I remember the days of old;
 I ponder all your deeds;
 the works of your hands I recall.
I stretch out my hands toward you,
 my soul to you like a parched land.
*Selah*
Hasten to answer me, LORD;
 for my spirit fails me.
Do not hide your face from me,
 lest I become like those descending to the pit.
In the morning let me hear of your mercy,
 for in you I trust.
Show me the path I should walk,
 for I entrust my life to you.
Rescue me, LORD, from my foes,
 for I seek refuge in you.
Teach me to do your will,
 for you are my God.
May your kind spirit guide me
 on ground that is level.
For your name's sake, LORD, give me life;
 in your righteousness lead my soul out of distress.
(Ps 143:1–11)

## REFLECT

If you didn't desire the Lord in some way, you wouldn't even be reading this book. But how common is it for us to say that we desire the Lord, and yet we do not act upon it?

The Lord is supposed to be our one desire. We sing songs and hear in the liturgy that our hearts are supposed to be totally his, but how true is it for each of us, really? Am I a hypocrite for saying these words when my life doesn't reflect this reality? If Jesus were truly my one desire, I would pursue him with my entire life, wouldn't I?

This is closer to the truth: I wish Jesus were my one desire. I want it, I do. I want to want to give myself totally to the Lord.

I know that true happiness, true fulfillment, true joy, and true peace can only come from God. I know that I am his daughter, and that he is my Father. I believe that trusting him and seeking him are what I am called to do. He gave everything for love of me, and he still calls me at every moment of every day. Yet, I fail to respond more often than not. Sometimes it's guilt that keeps me from responding to the Lord. Other times it's something physical that keeps me: I haven't had enough sleep, I've been overwhelmed with small people who need me all day, or I'm busy driving to soccer practice and volleyball games and piano lessons. But many, many times, what keeps me from responding to God is my lack of willpower during those small moments when I actually do have the time to pray.

Sometimes when I find myself so busy, the last thing I want to do is stop and pray. Even when I find myself having the time, I really just want to scroll on my phone or watch a funny video or read a book or take a nap. I wish that wasn't the case. I want to intentionally seek the Lord. I know that when I seek him, I will find him. If I knock, the door will be opened to me. There has never been a situation where I have regretted taking time to pray and encounter Jesus. But there have been many times when I have regretted wasting time or putting the wrong things at the top of my priorities.

In the garden of Gethsemane, Jesus prayed, "Father, if you are willing, take this cup away from me; still, not my will but yours be done" (Lk 22:42). Even Jesus wanted to want to do God's will. Even Jesus didn't want to do the greatest thing he ever did. And yet, he assented. He did it anyway. He put his own knee-jerk reaction aside and chose the higher thing, the better thing. You don't have to feel guilty for not wanting to pray. Not "feeling" it, not being sincere enough, not being in the right headspace, being distracted, having been lax in prayer in the past, or being unsure of a consistent commitment to prayer in the future—none of this should get in the way of choosing to meet the Lord in prayer today.

If prayer were easy, it wouldn't be an act of love. If we could pray on instinct, it wouldn't be a choice. But how many of us have truly regretted choosing to do an act of love?

Every day we get the opportunity to spend time with the Lord. We might prefer to catch up on our show, scroll social media, organize the Tupperware cabinet, or read a good book, but we will never regret using our time to sit with the Lord—even if we don't want to. I can't make myself desire prayer. I can't make myself feel anything that I don't feel. But I can still ask and seek and knock. I can still choose to be faithful to prayer, even when I don't desire it. And I know that I can ask the Lord to *help* me desire it, if it is his will that I do.

Here I am. I'm showing up. That has to count. I want to want to be intimate with the Lord.

## TAKE TO PRAYER

- Whether or not you feel a desire for God, why do you keep searching for him? Why are you reading this book?
- What habits would need to change in your life if you were to respond to God more intentionally throughout your day? Talk to God about your thoughts around your desire for prayer.

---

**PRAY WITH THIS LINE TODAY:**

Help me, Lord. I want to want you.

---

# DAY 2

# CASTING OFF OUR DISTRACTIONS

---

### IF YOU ONLY HAVE TWO MINUTES TO PRAY TODAY, PRAY THIS:

Lord, give me the willpower to resist the temptation of distraction from prayer. Give me a true love and desire for prayer, and help me to choose it today and every day. Amen.

---

## RECEIVE FROM THE WORD

As they continued their journey he entered a village where a woman whose name was Martha welcomed him. She had a sister named Mary [who] sat beside the Lord at his feet listening to him speak. Martha, burdened with much serving, came to him and said, "Lord, do you not care that my sister has left me by myself to do the serving? Tell her to help me." The Lord said to her in reply, "Martha, Martha, you are anxious and worried about many things. There is need of only one thing. Mary has chosen the better part and it will not be taken from her." (Lk 10:38–42)

# REFLECT

Have you ever been asked if you are a "Martha" or a "Mary"? My drive to have a clean home rather than a desire to pray in the midst of the mess definitely makes me a Martha. To be honest, though, I am not very good at cleaning my house. I have decided that I can either have happy, creative children or a nice, clean home. To have both at the same time seems impossible. While I don't relate to Martha's desire to have everything "just so," I do resonate with temptation for distraction when faced with an opportunity for prayer.

Consider Martha: Maybe she had prior notice that Jesus and his disciples were coming into town, and she just put off preparing until the last minute. Maybe she had no notice at all and was completely surprised at their visit—in which case, she would be scrambling to make sure there was enough seating in her home and enough water to go around. She may have wanted to prepare for all the things that make people feel welcome in her home. No matter the reason, we know she was scrambling and likely thinking, "What is Jesus going to think of my home? If it isn't comfortable enough, will he want to come back? I need to check all these things off my list and make sure that they're done before he gets here!"

And what was Mary doing this whole time? Maybe she was helping her sister prepare. But maybe she was in her room, preparing her heart to receive the Lord. Regardless, when Jesus showed up, she completely dismissed her concerns for household affairs. It's possible she was thinking about them in the back of her mind. She almost surely sensed her sister's frustration with her. Yet, she chose to sit at the Master's feet despite the temptation of distraction.

I, too, have many distractions. Not all of them are bad, which is why they're allowed a seat at the table. When God made us mothers, he knew we'd be busy. He knew that we would be preparing meals and wiping butts and breaking up fights between siblings. To be fair, though, some of the parts of motherhood that keep us busy are more important than others. Keeping the sink clean, feeding a sourdough starter, and folding laundry certainly benefit the household; doom scrolling and watching Netflix for "self-care" probably don't.

Whatever our distractions are, we've (maybe subconsciously) decided that they're necessary—for the function of the house, for our mental health, for our family's gut health, or a whole host of other reasons. And whatever we've prioritized in our lives takes up a certain amount of time in our day, a particular amount of willpower, and a share of our mental load. Seeking the Lord in daily prayer usually gets placed on the back burner to doing all these other things, good as they may be.

The Lord wants my "first fruits"—the best parts of myself—but usually ends up with the tired scraps of time and a reluctant attention span, if he gets any part of me at all.

In order to truly give myself to the Lord, I need to cast off these distractions and put him first. But these distractions are here for a reason: If they were easy to get rid of, I would have already moved past them. And here's the tricky part—a very real part of me does not want to cast them off. I like watching celebrities eat hot wings interview-style on YouTube and scrolling through funny reels on Instagram. And how will I know what happens on my thriller Netflix show if I don't watch it the night it comes out? Part of me tells myself these activities qualify as "self-care." So much of my life is not my own, so it only makes sense that I would use every spare moment to do something for myself. And yet, the Lord calls us to something higher.

I have a crystal-clear list of priorities for my family, but only a hazy, abstract idea of my priorities for my spiritual life. And that reality shakes me a little. God knew family life would be busy, but he also knew that it would still be possible to seek him amid and despite the busyness. Here's the trick we learn through faithfulness: When we give the Lord the firstfruits of ourselves, he gives us so much more in return. The Lord will not be outdone in generosity. As we are generous with our hearts and our priorities toward him, he will bring so much grace and goodness to our lives that will ultimately fulfill whatever it was we were seeking to begin with.

## TAKE TO PRAYER

- What does your schedule say about your priorities? What about your habits?
- What distracts you from seeking the Lord? Speak honestly to the Lord about the parts of yourself that are hard to hand over to Jesus.

---

**PRAY WITH THIS LINE TODAY:**

Transform me, Lord.
Help me set aside what is not of you.

---

## DAY 3

# WHERE IS THE LORD IN THIS?

### IF YOU ONLY HAVE TWO MINUTES TO PRAY TODAY, PRAY THIS:

Lord, where are you in this?
My reason tells me you're here, but it
can be so hard to feel you. Help me to
seek you in every moment today. Amen.

## RECEIVE FROM THE WORD

For I know well the plans I have in mind for you . . . plans for your welfare and not for woe, so as to give you a future of hope. When you call me, and come and pray to me, I will listen to you. When you look for me, you will find me. Yes, when you seek me with all your heart, I will let you find me . . . and I will change your lot. (Jer 29:11–14a)

## REFLECT

The human heart knows well the cry to the Lord. It's almost as if we were made for it. In the garden of Eden, when humanity walked intimately with the Lord, we knew for certain that he was there, present for us. Imagine for a minute what that relationship must have been like. Imagine being totally free to be exactly who God made you to be. It took no effort to hear and respond to God. Feel the fresh grass under your feet, the cool breeze bouncing off the water, refreshing your face. Imagine speaking intimately with the One who made you about anything and everything—his heart and yours totally open to each other. You could ask questions about who you are or about his creation, and he would answer in fullness and love, filling up your soul with the mysteries of who he is and who you are. There would be no shame or fear because there is nothing to be anxious about.

But God loves us so much that he gave us the gift of freedom, and we go astray. We were made for this kind of intimate relationship, once woven in love and trust and openness, but we inevitably corrupt it. We twist love into use. We warp trust into suspicion. We crush openness into shame. We are no longer sure of God's love and are doomed to forever question God's motives and feel abandoned by him.

But the story of our fall holds a crucial detail. After Adam and Eve sinned, they heard the Lord cry out, "Where are you?" (Gn 3:9). Even when we wander, the Lord calls out for us, asking us where we are!

The Lord is present in every situation, but it is hard to really believe that sometimes. We are constantly told that God knows every hair on our head, every grain of sand on the seashore. He knows every thought that we've ever had, and the desires that we've hidden in the depths of our hearts. But when we're busy, overwhelmed, or tired, the Lord's presence seems incredibly distant. We may find ourselves crying out to the Lord, "Where are you? Are you there? Do you care?" Or we may find ourselves forgetting to call out to the Lord at all, subconsciously preferring to absorb the stress or wallow in our own despair.

But even when we forget to call upon him, he is there. He is there with every gust of wind, with every rustle of the leaves. He is there when the sunlight streams through the windows, when my three-year-old covers her face with chalk, when I'm stuck in traffic. When I'm overwhelmed with thinking about the conversation I need to have with my husband, the Lord is with me. When I'm up in the middle of the night with the baby, the Lord is with me. When rolling my eyes at my teenager or holding my child's hair as they puke in the toilet, the Lord is with me.

When I was in grad school, I had a spiritual director who would ask, "Where is the Lord in this?" It was an incredibly frustrating question. Here I was, pouring my heart out in spiritual direction, wanting answers, desiring to know my next steps. I had no idea where the Lord was—and I didn't want to think about it, either. But that question was the most important question of my life. God wants us to stop spinning on the hamster wheels of our anxiety, to stop our panic and confusion, and simply to recognize that he is here. He is always present to us, even when we can't feel him near.

How different our lives would become if we allowed our hearts to yearn for heaven! How different I would be if I allowed the Lord to be present to me in my every moment! Even in the hard things. And the beautiful things. And the funny things. Life would be so much less lonely, so much less distracting. How much more full our lives would be if we knew we were walking with the Father who guides our every step.

## TAKE TO PRAYER

- Take a minute to put yourself in the presence of God. When distracting thoughts come, recognize them and allow them to pass.
- Talk to God about a way you experience his nearness. Recall a time when you were intimately aware of his presence. Where is the Lord showing up in your life today?

**PRAY WITH THIS LINE TODAY:**

Make me aware of your movement
and presence in everything, Lord.

## DAY 4

# LONGING TO HEAR FROM GOD

---

### IF YOU ONLY HAVE TWO MINUTES TO PRAY TODAY, PRAY THIS:

Lord, speak to me today. Open my heart to better perceive your presence. Help me listen for you, even within the distractions that come my way. And when you speak, let me recognize your voice. Amen.

---

## RECEIVE FROM THE WORD

The voice of the Lord is over the waters;
    the God of glory thunders,
    the Lord, over the mighty waters.
The voice of the Lord is power;
    the voice of the Lord is splendor.
The voice of the Lord cracks the cedars;
    the Lord splinters the cedars of Lebanon,

Makes Lebanon leap like a calf,
  and Sirion like a young bull.
The voice of the LORD strikes with fiery flame;
  the voice of the LORD shakes the desert;
  the LORD shakes the desert of Kadesh.
The voice of the LORD makes the deer dance
  and strips the forests bare.
  All in his Temple say, "Glory!"

The LORD sits enthroned above the flood!
  The LORD reigns as king forever!
May the LORD give might to his people;
  may the LORD bless his people with peace!
(Ps 29:3–11)

## REFLECT

Many years ago, an elderly man sat in prayer. He and his wife had done their best to raise their sons in a way that would please God, despite the fact that the city they lived in was notorious for sin. Their neighbors, friends, and even extended family could not understand why the man and his family chose to live in such a radically different way from everyone else they knew. They were ridiculed for it, and often excluded from social gatherings. But it was worth it, the man knew. He believed, in his heart, that God was pleased with him and his family. Even though he had never really heard from God in a radical way, he trusted that the suffering he had endured would be worth it. Until one day when everything changed.

God spoke to him and asked his family to do something truly radical—something that actually sounded crazy. Because of the relationship the man had built with God in prayer, he knew God's voice when he heard it, and he obeyed God's commands. So, in the middle of the desert community in which they lived, Noah and his family began to build a massive structure that would hold two of every living creature that breathed air upon the earth. God was with him, giving him instructions on how to build the ark step by step. After all these years of seeking God's will on earth despite opposition, finally Noah was actually hearing God give him specific instructions on what to do! How incredibly satisfying and vindicating! That euphoric feeling did not last, though.

As soon as the doors were shut and the rain came down, the Lord did not speak so clearly to Noah, according to scripture. Noah and his family were on the ark for more than a year. I wonder what Noah's prayer must have been like during that time. Did he wonder if the Lord was going to speak to him as clearly as before? Was he tempted to believe that the Lord had forgotten him? For forty days and nights it poured. The boat rocked. Was there fear or doubt in Noah's heart? Did he become discouraged in his own prayer? He must have been praying, "God, please tell me that we're going to be okay."

Silence from God in prayer is one of the top reasons we lack the desire to pray. How many times have I cried out to God about a situation and been met with radio silence? *Come in, base. Assistance needed. Mayday! Mayday! Assistance required immediately!* And seemingly nothing happens from the only source of my help. *Are you listening, Lord? I know you can hear me. Does that mean you're ignoring me? Is my problem too small, or too big, for you? Do you just not care?*

No, I know that he cares. I know that he listens. I know that he intends to come through for me, in some way. If the Lord did speak to me, though, would I listen? Do I even know what his voice sounds like?

It's hard to hear the voice of the Lord when there are so many other voices competing for my attention. Some of these voices have been given to me for my care—my husband and children, for instance. And these are people who truly need me and who need me to respond. But there are other voices to whom I lend my ear—some are distractions of the world, and some are distractions from the evil one. Sometimes it's my own voice that crowds out the voice of the Lord in my heart. But I want to hear from the Lord! I deeply desire to hear his voice, what he wants to say to me and speak into my life. His words are full of life and bring life to my soul. I want to push back all the other unnecessary voices and keep my heart and mind for the voice of the Lord.

It's not that God doesn't want to talk to me—it's that I don't know how to listen to him. When he speaks, I don't recognize his voice. I don't make the space in my life to hear what he has to say. But I want to recognize it when I hear his voice. I want to breathe in his Word and walk in his presence. When I am surrounded by voices, both good and bad, I want to know what the Lord says. The most important voice I'll ever hear in my entire life will be the voice of the One who spoke the universe into being. And he speaks to me, even when I'm not listening.

I imagine Noah begging to hear from God while being tossed and turned in the boat. And God, who had never left, was speaking and present in the drops of rain, in the splash of water, in the powerful howling of the wind, and in the silence of the night.

## TAKE TO PRAYER

- When is the last time you felt as if God was clearly speaking to you? What did he say, and how did you perceive him saying it?
- If God does not speak to you in a way that you can discern with words, what are some other ways you might be able to hear his voice in your life? Take a minute to listen to the Lord. Write down what you hear, feel, or sense.

---

**PRAY WITH THIS LINE TODAY:**

Speak, Lord, for your servant is listening.

---

# DAY 5

# DESIRE FOR TRANSFORMATION

---

### IF YOU ONLY HAVE TWO MINUTES TO PRAY TODAY, PRAY THIS:

Who did you create me to be? I am but clay in your hands, Lord. Mold me, shape me, and transform me into the person you want me to be. Amen.

---

## RECEIVE FROM THE WORD

This word came to Jeremiah from the LORD: Arise and go down to the potter's house; there you will hear my word. I went down to the potter's house and there he was, working at the wheel. Whenever the vessel of clay he was making turned out badly in his hand, he tried again, making another vessel of whatever sort he pleased. Then the word of the LORD came to me: Can I not do to you, house of Israel, as this potter has done? . . . Indeed, like clay in the

> hand of the potter, so are you in my hand, house of Israel. (Jer 18:1–6)

## REFLECT

I know that life lived in a casual commitment to Jesus is not the fullness of what God wants for me. God's plan for me is so much greater than any plan or dream I might have for myself. There's a part of me that does want to live for him alone, but there is fear and reluctance to do what is necessary to give myself totally to God. I need to choose this transformation in my life, even if it means giving up something I don't want to give up, even if it means changing my life in a radical way. I want to go where the Lord is calling me, even when it doesn't make any sense to the rest of the world.

In John's gospel, Jesus meets a Samaritan woman drawing water from a well in the heat of the day. Knowing that no one else would be around to ridicule her or exclude her because of her sinful life choices, the woman decides it's better to just suffer in the noon heat alone than to suffer the stares and comments of her neighbors who draw water in the cool of the morning. Jesus confronts her and asks for a drink. The woman is shocked that a man, a Jewish man, would even acknowledge her presence, as Jews generally went out of their way to avoid Samaritans. And Jesus responds that if she knew who he was, it would be she who would ask him for a drink. As the confused woman continues to protest, Jesus gives us a beautiful illustration of his plan for grace. He offers her living water and promises that if she were to drink of it, she would never be thirsty again because it would become a spring of eternal life. The woman is intrigued at the prospect of never being thirsty again (and never needing to face the other women at the well, who would remind her of her sin) but is even more shocked as Jesus tells her the sins she has committed and is currently committing.

Notice something here, though: Jesus offers the Samaritan woman a drink of eternal life, of his grace, before the woman has even repented—before she has even admitted her sinfulness! Even as she asks for this drink with shame in her heart, Jesus's love and gentleness and eagerness to redeem her shine light upon the truth that she lives in every day. And it works. The woman is transformed into someone new. She becomes Jesus's best evangelist in Samaria, telling everyone about his love and mercy. If Jesus can transform a sinful woman who can't imagine the new life he is offering, how much more can he transform me?

There is something about the word *thirst* that draws us in. When we think of what it means to be thirsty, a very physical reaction begins in our bodies. Thirst includes a dry sensation in our mouths; we can feel it on our tongue, in the crack of our lips, and on the roof of our mouths. We might even get a bit of a desperate feeling if it's been a while since we've drunk anything. We can feel it in our arms and in our toes, this desire to consume something that we know we need. The Lord wants us to feel that thirst more acutely in our souls than in our mouths: a thirst not for drink, but for holiness, for transformation. He wants us to desire transformation more than we desire comfort, or health, or the good opinions of others.

What does it mean to be transformed? It means I am no longer my own. It means I am like the clay Jeremiah witnessed, and the Lord is the potter. It means I let the Lord put me on the potter's wheel and spin me around and around until I have taken the shape that he has designed. It may also mean giving the Lord permission to stick me into the refiner's fire to burn away all the impurities and imperfections so that I can shine like gold. This process is jarring, to say the least. I'm scared to ask the Lord to refine me. But I also need to ask: Am I so scared of being purified that I risk losing out on God's design for my life?

What good is the life we've dreamed of if we're not living the life God wants for us? It's hard to know where to start, to be honest. So let's start here: What is God calling me to right now? What does he want in the present moment? Past sin can't stop us: Jesus wants to take that sin and throw it far away from us, as far as the east is from the west. There's no better time to start praying for transformation than right now.

## TAKE TO PRAYER

- What needs to be transformed in your life? If each moment is a path to holiness, where are you being led right now?
- What parts of your life need more attention as opportunities for grace?
- What would your life look like if you were radically faithful to the Lord? What stops you from turning your life over to God?

---

**PRAY WITH THIS LINE TODAY:**

Transform my thirst into something more.
Help me love you more.

---

## DAY 6

# COME, HOLY SPIRIT!

---

### IF YOU ONLY HAVE TWO MINUTES TO PRAY TODAY, PRAY THIS:

Come, Holy Spirit, fill the hearts of your faithful and kindle in them the fire of your love. Send forth your Spirit and they shall be created, and you shall renew the face of the earth. Amen.

---

## RECEIVE FROM THE WORD

And I tell you, ask and you will receive; seek and you will find; knock and the door will be opened to you. For everyone who asks, receives; and the one who seeks, finds; and to the one who knocks, the door will be opened. What father among you would hand his son a snake when he asks for a fish? Or hand him a scorpion when he asks for an egg? If you then, who are wicked, know how to give good gifts to your children, how much more will the Father in heaven give the holy Spirit to those who ask him? (Lk 11:9–13)

## REFLECT

What is the Holy Spirit? Perhaps a better question to ask would be "who" rather than "what." The Holy Spirit is not a dove, despite the insistence of every nineties Vacation Bible School session or religious-education class. The Holy Spirit is a person, one with whom we can have a relationship. Not only that, but the Holy Spirit is the One who responds to our prayers when we ask for help and guidance, for courage and strength. We can have an intimate relationship with this forgotten member of the Trinity—if only we remember to call upon the Spirit.

We have heard that Jesus did not come for the righteous, but for sinners. But do we realize that he also did not come just for those with ample prayer time, but for those whose lives are in chaos? In fact, the first place we see evidence of the workings of the Holy Spirit is in the very beginning of the Bible. The first chapter of Genesis gives us the story of creation and the state of the universe before the Lord created light: "In the beginning, when God created the heavens and the earth—and the earth was without form or shape, with darkness over the abyss and a mighty wind sweeping over the waters" (1:1–2). This "mighty wind" is the first glimpse we get of the Holy Spirit. Before creation, there was nothing but disorder and chaos—an abyss. Then something happens: Power. Might. The Holy Spirit passes through the abyss, the chaos, to prepare it for something beautiful. The very next verse is the most famous verse in Genesis: "Then God said: Let there be light" (1:3).

This verse alone is a love letter from God to parents. The Holy Spirit is for you. A life of holiness is for you! In fact, you are his priority! The first thing the Holy Spirit does is to enter into the chaos and disorder and prepare it for beauty and wonder. The Holy Spirit desires to enter your life, as chaotic and disorderly as it may be, and he will make it beautiful. Just as there will be more rejoicing in heaven over one sinner who repents, nothing gives the Holy Spirit more pleasure than to enter chaos.

I know that if I ask for the Holy Spirit, he will come. This is one of Jesus's most powerful promises—that he will send the Holy Spirit to those who ask! But how often do I actually take the time to ask? How often do I call upon the Holy Spirit? And if the Holy Spirit came, would I recognize him? If all I have to do is ask, then here I am, asking. If all I have to do is knock, then here I am, knocking. The Holy Spirit is the giver of every good gift. I want that in my life! I want to receive the Spirit's help in every situation. I want to use the gifts of the Spirit to edify my family. I want to live a life of holiness with the fruits of the Holy Spirit. I can't earn the presence of the Holy Spirit, but I can cry out for the Spirit to come live inside me.

I don't know how the Holy Spirit wants to move in my life, but I know the Spirit wants to do something incredible. I don't know what gifts the Spirit intends to give me, but I know that whatever they are, they will change my life. I don't know how the Spirit wants to move in my life, but I am open to whatever it is. The apostles' lives were completely transformed when they received the Holy Spirit—and the Spirit wants to transform my life too. The Giver of Gifts is ready to give. Am I ready to receive? All I need to do is to make myself open and available to receive these gifts and simply ask the Spirit to come. It's really that simple.

When we invite the Holy Spirit into our lives, something objectively changes—even if we don't feel it. During those days when we feel nothing, God is inviting us to be persistent. Keep asking, keep seeking, keep knocking. And the door will be opened to us.

## TAKE TO PRAYER

- What is your relationship with the Holy Spirit like? What would you like it to be?
- What gifts or fruits of the Spirit do you desire? Ask the Lord how he wants to transform you through the Holy Spirit.

## PRAY WITH THIS LINE TODAY:

Come, Holy Spirit!
Come into my life today.

# DAY 7

# O THAT YOU WOULD REND THE HEAVENS!

---

### IF YOU ONLY HAVE TWO MINUTES TO PRAY TODAY, PRAY THIS:

O that you would rend the heavens and come down, Lord! I was made to desire you; every need and desire that I have was made to be filled by you. Fill me, Lord, with your presence. Amen.

---

## RECEIVE FROM THE WORD

As the deer longs for streams of water,
    so my soul longs for you, O God.
My soul thirsts for God, the living God.
    When can I enter and see the face of God?
My tears have been my bread day and night,
    as they ask me every day, "Where is your God?"
Those times I recall

as I pour out my soul,
When I would cross over to the shrine of the Mighty One,
to the house of God,
Amid loud cries of thanksgiving,
with the multitude keeping festival.
Why are you downcast, my soul;
why do you groan within me?
Wait for God, for I shall again praise him,
my savior and my God.
(Ps 42:2–6)

## REFLECT

What an odd experience the Israelites must have had as they fled slavery in Egypt, traveling in the desert behind pillars of smoke and fire (Ex 13:21). Watching the sea being parted in two and walking across it. Being sustained every day by odd flakes that fell from the sky six days a week. And all this after witnessing the plagues that spared them and their families, while selectively torturing the Egyptians.

I tell myself that if I were there and witnessed it all, I would never want to sin again—the evidence of an all-powerful God who was intent on saving me and destroying his enemies would be too great. And yet, the Israelites seemed intent on sinning and turning their backs on God. Are you serious, Israelites? Bad move! If I was the Lord, I would have replaced this stiff-necked people a long time ago—I'll tell you that for free. Surely another nation or tribe would have been better at keeping covenants. But luckily I am not the Lord.

Why would the Lord choose such a stubborn people to be his? Why wouldn't he just give up on them and find a more grateful people to be his light to the nations—his chosen ones? He knew all of their choices before he made his covenant with them through Abraham. Why make the covenant if he knew they couldn't keep it?

Part of me thinks it's because of the desperate hearts of the Israelites. Consistently finding themselves in trouble (often of their own making), they cry out to the Lord even when they turn their backs on him. Even David, the king who committed adultery and murder, desperately cries out to the Lord God in every situation. And he is a "man after [God's] own heart" (1 Sm 13:14). There is a desperate longing that the Israelites exhibit (which sometimes manifests in a sinful direction, but it is longing nonetheless) that the Lord wants us to take notice of. He wants us to see these people and the longing they have in their hearts and to emulate it.

My family desperately needs God. No matter the day, the year, or the situation we find ourselves in—God is the source of all goodness, all mercy, all strength. He sustains us and nourishes us and keeps us going. We can do nothing without him, even when we forget to lean on him. I need all that he gives. I need the redemption and peace that he offers. I need the safety of his arms, his reassurance that it's going to be all right, and his strength when it's not going to be all right.

But most of all, I need his presence. He walks with me to the car while my hands are full, and he is with me while I'm at the dreaded parent-teacher conference. He comforts me when the pregnancy test is negative. He leaps with joy with me when my kid scores the winning point. He guides my hands while I'm experimenting with a new recipe or cleaning the vomit out of the car seat. I need him, not only for what he gives me, but for himself. I need him for his own sake, which is goodness itself.

It is the presence of the Lord that sustains me and gives me life. And I desire more! I desire more of his presence! I echo Isaiah, who cries out for the presence and glory of God: "O that you would rend the heavens and come down, [Lord]" (Is 63:19). I want God to break open heaven and earth and fix it all. Heaven seems so far away, and this life can make me weary. There is so much good in life because God made all things good. But there is also a weariness here, because this place is not what we are preparing for. A perfectly curated, Pinterest-worthy home is not the goal—heaven is. And so it makes sense that we will be restless, always striving, always seeking. Our souls were made for communion and intimacy with God, which can only be reflected imperfectly here.

And yet, our souls still long for the Lord. Like an itch we can't scratch, we will always be discontent until we find our rest in God. We have the Eucharist to sustain us on our journey, to keep us from withering away in indifference. But life continually reminds us: We are not in heaven—but how we long for it!

## TAKE TO PRAYER

- How do you notice a perpetual longing or discontent in your life? How can you redirect that dissatisfaction toward a longing for heaven?
- How might you become "desperate for God"? Talk to the Lord about how you need him to be present in your life.

---

**PRAY WITH THIS LINE TODAY:**

I need you, God—
you sustain me and give me life.

---

# WEEK 2: ENCOUNTER

My first memorable encounter with God was during adoration as a high schooler at a Steubenville youth conference. Before walking into the large auditorium at the University of Arizona for adoration, our youth minister gave us an odd tip: "When adoration starts, no matter what happens, don't look behind you." What? What's going to happen at adoration? I definitely had a feeling that this was going to be interesting.

The lights turned down, and musicians began to play worship songs. A spotlight followed the priest as he processed in so that people could see the Eucharist in the monstrance clearly. I remembered we weren't supposed to look behind us, so I didn't—but I could see the movement of the monstrance by following the movement of the spotlight.

And behind me I heard people crying, screaming. They were praying and singing in tongues, laughing, crying out their sins, and asking for forgiveness. I had never heard anything like that before in my life. Suddenly I knew why my youth minister had told us not to look behind us. The tangible presence of Christ was sweeping the room and we young, broken teens were reacting appropriately to an encounter with the eternal God. I was committed to staring at the musicians, trying to ignore the supernatural movement that was happening behind me. At some point, it became impossible to ignore.

I looked up at the position of the spotlight. I saw it pointing right behind me on the stairs next to my left. "It wouldn't hurt," I thought, "to just look behind real quick, just to see." So I looked. And God was standing on those steps. Now, to clarify, physically it looked just like a priest holding a monstrance with the Eucharist in it. But in that moment, the Lord removed the veil from my eyes and allowed me to see him as he is—in his glory, his beauty, his terror, his might. In an instant, I saw how beautiful and powerful and holy he was—and I saw how lowly and small and dirty I was, even though I wasn't a bad kid. (To be honest, I did cheat on a spelling test once in the second grade, but I felt so bad about it that I never did it again.)

At that moment, I saw the great chasm between myself and God—between his holiness and purity and my lowliness and unworthiness. At the same time, the Lord showed me that while, yes, he is holy and I am lowly, he still loves me so, so much. He loves me so much that he humbled himself to become a baby for me; so much that he died for me; so much that he uses bread and wine to nourish me with his very Body and Blood; so much that he lets me consume him every day at Mass! I fell to my knees in awe and repentance and bawled. I was so small—and yet so loved. I offered new true, desperate prayers of encounter: "Forgive me, Lord!" and "Thank you, Jesus!" and "I love you, Jesus!"

Week two of our journey begins with leaning into the transformative power of God as we meet him heart-to-heart. These encounters may be incredibly palpable like mine was, or barely perceptible. His presence, his voice, his gaze change us in ways that we cannot begin to fathom. Even if you're not sure if you've ever had an encounter with the living God, I guarantee that the Lord has been moving and working in your life. What would happen if we grew our capacity to recognize that encounter *as it was happening*? How would our lives change if we were better at perceiving the action, the movement, and the presence of God in our everyday lives?

St. Paul knew that Christ is with us at every moment because he is the ground of reality. He wrote:

> For in him were created all things in heaven and on earth,
> the visible and the invisible,
> whether thrones or dominions or principalities or powers;
> all things were created through him and for him.
> He is before all things,
> and in him all things hold together.
> (Col 1:16–17)

God is *being* itself. The fact that we exist means that he is constantly aware of us and constantly sustaining us. This truth is reflected in Jesus's very name: *Emmanuel* means "God with us."

God's loving presence saturates our world and our lives, and he invites us to step off of the hamster wheel of our daily concerns and notice. Do you see the light refracting across the window? That's God trying to get your attention. Do you feel the breeze from the fan overhead? That's the Lord's breath, blowing life into your lungs. Do you feel the comfort of your chair, the fuzz from your socks, the softness of your clothing on your shoulders? To delight in our createdness is to meet the Lord reaching for us. And yet, all these things are ordinary experiences that are so common that we don't even notice them.

What would happen if you did notice more, though? What would happen to your life if you found ways to more deeply encounter the living God, who is being itself, right where you are—here and now—even as you read these words with this book in your hands? He is constantly communicating his love to us, madly trying to get our attention!

When I consider this challenge—which is the aim of every strain of Christian spirituality—I realize I could live my life more intentionally. I might find deep, profound love in smaller moments throughout the day. I might parent my children more gracefully and act with thoughtfulness instead of reacting with emotion. Every sacrifice I make throughout the day might be done more joyfully and in union with Jesus—instead of offering it with a grumble because someone needs me to do it.

An encounter with Christ does not need to include a supernatural experience—in fact, he usually doesn't appear with parted clouds and a "Hallelujah" chorus. Remember: The first three decades of Jesus's life on earth were spent in the ordinary. And each person he encountered during those years before his public ministry began still truly encountered him. He proves to us that he can be found in the ordinary, quiet, hidden moments of our lives—moments that us moms know all too well. But make no mistake, every encounter with Christ does include a supernatural shift within ourselves. Every time I encounter Jesus, I become transformed. I am no longer the same.

This week, lean into an encounter with Jesus in every moment. Look for and notice his presence. Let him speak to you—if not in words, then simply in the spirit of his presence.

## TAKE TO PRAYER

- Spend a minute telling the Lord how you desire to encounter him this week.
- Leave quiet space to listen for his response.

## WATCH AND LISTEN

To watch a video introduction to this week, scan the QR code or visit www.avemariapress.com/pages/sacred-chaos-resources. You'll also find there a playlist with music to accompany your daily prayer.

## DAY 8

# ALIVE IN ME

### IF YOU ONLY HAVE TWO MINUTES TO PRAY TODAY, PRAY THIS:

Lord, I believe you are with me, here and now! You are living and moving within me, even when I can't feel you. Bring me to life today. Help me recognize your presence in every moment. Amen.

## RECEIVE FROM THE WORD

Come and assemble, gather together,
you fugitives from among the nations!
They are without knowledge who bear wooden idols
and pray to gods that cannot save.
Come close and declare;
let them take counsel together:
Who announced this from the beginning,
declared it from of old?

Was it not I, the LORD,
besides whom there is no other God?
There is no just and saving God but me.

Turn to me and be safe,
all you ends of the earth,
for I am God; there is no other!
By myself I swear,
uttering my just decree,
a word that will not return:
To me every knee shall bend;
by me every tongue shall swear,
Saying, "Only in the LORD
are just deeds and power.
Before him in shame shall come
all who vent their anger against him.
In the LORD all the descendants of Israel
shall have vindication and glory."
(Is 45:20–25)

## REFLECT

The Lord is here! The fact that you are even here, holding this book and searching for God in prayer, is proof that the Holy Spirit is moving and alive in you. That nudge you felt to pick up this book is what the prompting of the Spirit feels like. The simple yes you gave to carving out some time to be with the Lord today is proof of his movement in your life. The time you have—however much time that may be—was set aside for you by God himself.

Further, it's not just that God is outside of you, encouraging and nudging and speaking to you. Jesus is *alive in you*! He is not a dead historical figure of the past, or an over-simplified religious icon—he is truly God, and we are truly made for him. All of your soul, your mind, and your heart were made to be in communion with him. It's why nothing else in the world seems to satisfy. No social status, no relationship, no amount of money or social media followers can possibly give us what our hearts are searching for as we hungrily leap from distraction to distraction, worshipping the idol of the day.

There is a brilliant story in the Old Testament that, for some reason, has never made it into any children's collection of Bible stories. First Samuel 4–5 tells of a battle where the Philistines captured the ark of the covenant—the physical object that contained the Ten Commandments, and which the Lord had deemed appropriate to fill with his presence. The Philistines, knowing that the ark "contained" the God of Israel, foolishly placed it in a temple with their primary god, Dagon, a "fish god" depicted as half-man and half-fish.

The passages of 1 Samuel 5 reveal that though the two were placed side by side, the next morning Dagon was found on the ground with his face in the dirt. How fitting for a false fish god! The Lord was sending a message to the Philistines—he was saying, "I am alive. This thing is not. And to prove it to you, I will place your fish in the environment that is most detrimental to its kind: the dust."

The Philistines didn't get the message, however. They picked up Dagon and put him back in the temple. The following morning, Dagon was once again found face down in the dirt—this time with his head and hands cut off. It was enough to scare the Philistines out of entering the temple, but not enough to inspire them to return the ark. For the next seven months, the ark of the covenant was shuffled from city to city, leaving death and sickness in its wake, before it was voluntarily returned to the Israelites.

The Philistines knew that the ark had some sort of power; but they had no idea that the Lord was Lord of all. Dagon was made by a woodworker, crafted with nail and chisel. To say that this god was "dead" is not quite right, though—because in order to be dead, something must have first had life. This false god was an inanimate object from the start, incapable of knowing, thinking, or feeling—let alone being able to do anything about the prayers directed to it.

But the Lord is alive! Not only is he alive, he truly knows my heart and cares for what is in it. He truly knows what I was made for—because he made *me*. He gave me all my talents, my personality, and my silly quirks, and he has molded me to be me. Not only that, but he knows my limitations. He knows my baggage and my fears and insecurities. He knows when I feel stupid for thinking I'm talking to the air when I'm trying to pray, or when I feel guilty about that sinful habit, or when my patience is running low with the kids because can't I just have five minutes of peace for crying out loud? He knows all this—and yet, he lives in me! He isn't repelled by me at all. In fact, he loves that I've come to this moment looking to encounter him—even with unwashed hair and dirt under my fingernails.

Jesus is not so far away—he lives within me and is always moving, working, and healing. When I feel his presence, I know that it is a gift. When I don't feel his presence, I am faithful anyway. The Lord desires to make himself known, so here I am, listening and looking for him with faith that he is near.

## TAKE TO PRAYER

- Call to mind the last time you had a moving encounter with God. Relive those sweet moments and relish the memory of God's nearness.
- How are you encountering God today? What can you do to make yourself more aware of his presence?
- Remember: Jesus is alive in your heart! What does he see there? What does he say?

---

**PRAY WITH THIS LINE TODAY:**

Here I am, Lord! Consume me with your love.

---

## DAY 9

# THE REFINER'S FIRE

---

### IF YOU ONLY HAVE TWO MINUTES TO PRAY TODAY, PRAY THIS:

Purify me, Lord! I know that no one encounters you, the Creator of heaven and earth, and is left unchanged. Give me the courage and humility to submit to your purifying action in my life. Make me more like you every day. Amen.

---

## RECEIVE FROM THE WORD

A clean heart create for me, God;
  renew within me a steadfast spirit.
Do not drive me from before your face,
  nor take from me your holy spirit.
Restore to me the gladness of your salvation;
  uphold me with a willing spirit.
(Ps 51:12–14)

# REFLECT

Meeting God face-to-face, heart-to-heart, is a purifying experience. There is no way we can approach the Lord without having been changed in some way. As the refiner places gold into a furnace of fire to bring the impurities to the surface, the Lord also brings to the surface things that are uncomfortable or unpleasant. It's human nature to want to suppress our uncomfortable memories and ignore our faults. Yet, God wants us to approach him, no matter how many of those faults we have. But he also does not intend to leave us as he found us. He wants to redeem those broken parts of us that keep us far from him.

When Moses descended Mount Sinai after encountering God in the burning bush and receiving the Ten Commandments, his face was radiant. The experience radically changed him, which was even reflected in his appearance. The radiance of his face made the Israelites uneasy, so Moses wore a veil. But why would the Israelites be disturbed in looking upon Moses's face? Moses's encounter with God had made him holy, and the people knew it—his appearance revealed to them how far they were, themselves, from God's presence. Coming face-to-face with holiness can convict us to reorient our lives, or it can make us want to bury our sin deeper in the darkness.

It's no wonder that the Lord continually uses fire and light to describe his purifying and transformative action: Light reveals. It makes hidden things known. The Lord wants to illuminate what lies hidden in the dark corners of our lives—he wants to bring us into the light. As we encounter him, he wants us to bare our hearts to him. We don't have to fix ourselves or have a ten-point plan to improve what's broken and wounded in us—we just have to present our whole selves to him, and God will do the rest. That's the good news about encountering Jesus: He does the work to make us whole. We just have to be vulnerable enough to let him do it.

Will I fight against his purifying action and resist what he wants to do in my life? Or will I take a big breath, close my eyes, and let the One who loves me purify me in ways I did not know I could be purified?

## TAKE TO PRAYER

- What sins do you struggle with the most? Talk to God about them. What does he say about them?
- Taking those faults to Confession reinforces God's mercy. When is the next opportunity you could experience that sacrament?
- How can your encounter with the Lord today serve as a step in your journey to holiness—and what might be your next step?

---

### PRAY WITH THIS LINE TODAY:

Jesus, give me the courage to sit
in your refiner's fire. Make me holy.

---

## DAY 10

# I BREATHE YOU IN

---

### IF YOU ONLY HAVE TWO MINUTES TO PRAY TODAY, PRAY THIS:

You are here, God—all around me,
within me, near me, through me.
Your presence fills up every space.
Help me know you are with me today.
Amen.

---

## RECEIVE FROM THE WORD

Lord, you have probed me, you know me:
    you know when I sit and stand;
    you understand my thoughts from afar.
You sift through my travels and my rest;
    with all my ways you are familiar.
Even before a word is on my tongue,
    Lord, you know it all.
Behind and before you encircle me
    and rest your hand upon me.

Such knowledge is too wonderful for me,
    far too lofty for me to reach.

Where can I go from your spirit?
    From your presence, where can I flee?
If I ascend to the heavens, you are there;
    if I lie down in Sheol, there you are.
If I take the wings of dawn
    and dwell beyond the sea,
Even there your hand guides me,
    your right hand holds me fast.
If I say, "Surely darkness shall hide me,
    and night shall be my light"—
Darkness is not dark for you,
    and night shines as the day.
    Darkness and light are but one.
(Ps 139:1–12)

## REFLECT

The presence of the Lord is a mystery. On one hand, God is totally omnipotent and omnipresent. He is in us and with us, closer than anyone else could be—closer than we are to ourselves. He sustains our lives. And yet, we have not fully realized what it means to be in complete communion with him as we would in heaven. We are living in the "now" and "not yet."

Breath is fundamental to life. As we breathe in, oxygen fills up our lungs and travels through the bronchioles, into the little alveoli sacs that convey oxygen to our bodies through our hearts. That same oxygen we breathe in is now pumped through our entire body, giving muscles what they need to contract and relax, allowing the brain to fuel nerve cells. As we breathe, many processes are happening that sustain us and give us life—and yet, it's as natural as . . . well, breathing. We don't even notice this life-giving process, but it sustains us just the same.

We read in Genesis that God "breathed" upon Adam and gave him life and a soul (2:7). That first breath of humanity was literally God's breath. It's a beautiful image of the way we were made in God's image and likeness. Our souls—our capacity to choose, our reason, our ability to love—come from a mighty breath given to no other creature. But I also wonder, What was Adam's second breath like? It clearly was not the identity-altering, reality-shattering event of that first breath—but it was just as necessary. Each breath we take is enough to sustain us for a few moments. It rushes through our bodies and fills up our lungs, our hearts, our blood vessels. But then we must breathe again to stretch our lives into the next moment. With each succeeding breath, God continues to fill us with his presence, to give us life even when we are in sin or when we're distracted.

The author of Genesis used the word *ruah*, or "breath," to describe God's power in the act of creation (2:7)—he literally breathed the world into being. This same breath is a life-giving movement of God in our bodies. God's presence is so tangible and immanent that he can be found with every breath we take. Like our breath, we can perceive him when we let ourselves think about it. But even when we aren't aware of him, he is still faithfully present to us, sustaining us and bringing us life.

The Lord is here, even when we cannot feel him. He is here in the laughter of my children. In the car line. In the football stands. In the kitchen, as I wonder what to cook for dinner. In the baby's smile. As I hear the hum of the TV in the background. He is ever present, inviting me to stop, to close my eyes, and to breathe him in.

## TAKE TO PRAYER

- Close your eyes and notice your breath. Imagine you are breathing in the presence of God. Regardless of whether or not you feel his presence, how does knowing he is near change your outlook?
- What is the Lord doing in your heart in this moment, right now?

How can you turn your mind to acknowledge his presence throughout the day today?

---

**PRAY WITH THIS LINE TODAY:**

I breathe you in, Lord.

---

## DAY 11

# YOUR WORDS ARE LIFE

---

**IF YOU ONLY HAVE TWO MINUTES TO PRAY TODAY, PRAY THIS:**

Lord, you are speaking to me at every moment. Even when I cannot discern what those words are, I know that your voice is leading me to life and love. Help me to hear your voice today, and to listen well. Amen.

---

## RECEIVE FROM THE WORD

Amen, amen, I say to you, whoever hears my word and believes in the one who sent me has eternal life and will not come to condemnation, but has passed from death to life. Amen, amen, I say to you, the hour is coming and is now here when the dead will hear the voice of the Son of God, and those who hear will live. For just as the Father has life in himself, so also he gave to his Son the possession of life in himself. And he gave him power to exercise judgment, because he is the Son of Man. Do not be amazed

> at this, because the hour is coming in which all who are in the tombs will hear his voice and will come out, those who have done good deeds to the resurrection of life, but those who have done wicked deeds to the resurrection of condemnation. (Jn 5:24–29)

## REFLECT

How do we hear God's voice? What are we listening for? The Bible offers a compelling story from the experience of Elijah, who heard God speaking to him in quiet stillness.

Elijah's life was in danger, and he was in despair. The Lord, ever patient, told him to go to a mountain and promised to pass by him to console him with his presence. The first book of Kings tells what happened next: "There was a strong and violent wind rending the mountains and crushing rocks before the LORD—but the LORD was not in the wind; after the wind, an earthquake—but the LORD was not in the earthquake; after the earthquake, fire—but the LORD was not in the fire; after the fire, a light silent sound. When he heard this, Elijah hid his face in his cloak and went out and stood at the entrance of the cave" (19:11–13).

Elijah feared for his life because he had just stood up to an evil queen and confronted her false god. He revealed the power of the living God in a dramatic, miraculous scene. So Elijah knew the power of God. But it was not the power of God that Elijah needed to see just then, in his moment of great fear for his life. It was the quiet gentleness of God that he needed. He needed to see that the Lord's strength does not merely lie in a physical display of wonder and awe; he needed to see that the Lord cares for him and his heart. Elijah, having spent enough time communicating and speaking with God, knew what the voice of the Lord sounded like, whether it was in a display of dramatic power or in a still voice. He knew how to find God's presence in intimate silence.

As the story continues, we see that God knew Elijah's limits and told him to appoint a successor: Elisha. God wasn't just gentle in speech, but he was also gentle in how he led Elijah's life. The Lord knew exactly what Elijah needed and how to say it to him—and he provided. God is faithful!

How do we know what the Lord is saying? What does he say to us? The best way to find out is to practice attending to the presence of God. The more time we spend in his presence, the more aware of his movements we are. And when we recognize his movements, we begin to recognize what his voice sounds like—what he is saying to us through the circumstances of our lives. Sometimes, the Lord does say something tangible or decipherable that we understand with language. But many, many times, his voice is not discernible in the kind of words that we are used to. So many times, his voice is the soft, gentle whisper of love. It is a gentle reminder that he is still doing and moving and working and filling us with his loving presence.

When my teenager rolls her eyes, he speaks. When I'm going through school emails, he speaks. At every baseball game, swim meet, and band concert, he speaks. When my toddler is inexplicably screaming because she got exactly the lunch meal she asked for, he speaks. When my kid loses his first tooth, he speaks. When I'm up with the baby at 3 a.m. again, he speaks. And he speaks in the way I most need to hear him and provides for my every need. His words give me life.

## TAKE TO PRAYER

- When is the last time you felt or heard the Lord speaking to you? If it was discernible in words, what did he say? If it was more of a conclusion or feeling, how were you able to hear him?
- What mode of prayer makes it easier for you to hear from the Lord? How can you incorporate that practice into your daily life?
- What do you feel the Lord is speaking to you now?

## PRAY WITH THIS LINE TODAY:

Your word, O Lord, is life.
Speak, for I am listening.

## DAY 12

# TASTE AND SEE

### IF YOU ONLY HAVE TWO MINUTES TO PRAY TODAY, PRAY THIS:

Lord, to whom else shall I go?
For you have the words of eternal life.
Satisfy me, O God! Amen.

## RECEIVE FROM THE WORD

"I am the bread of life. Your ancestors ate the manna in the desert, but they died; this is the bread that comes down from heaven so that one may eat it and not die. I am the living bread that came down from heaven; whoever eats this bread will live forever; and the bread that I will give is my flesh for the life of the world."

The Jews quarreled among themselves, saying, "How can this man give us [his] flesh to eat?" Jesus said to them, "Amen, amen, I say to you, unless you eat the flesh of the Son of Man and drink his blood, you do not have life within you. Whoever eats my flesh and drinks my blood has

> eternal life, and I will raise him on the last day. For my flesh is true food, and my blood is true drink. Whoever eats my flesh and drinks my blood remains in me and I in him. Just as the living Father sent me and I have life because of the Father, so also the one who feeds on me will have life because of me. This is the bread that came down from heaven. Unlike your ancestors who ate and still died, whoever eats this bread will live forever." (Jn 6:48–58)

## REFLECT

More than two thousand years ago, a young, pregnant woman and her husband were searching for a place to rest as she began her labor. The usually quiet town was noisy that night, as travelers gathered their belongings and met up with distant relatives. This town, which was also known as the "House of Bread," became the birthplace for the Bread of Life: Jesus Christ. As an exhausted Mary laid her son in a feed trough for animals, the tiny Lord willingly let himself take the place of food that sustains beasts of burden. I wonder how many animals came up to their trough expecting to feed on grain while the Bread of Life lay in the manger.

None of these details happened by accident. From the first moment of the beginning of salvation history, God was sustaining us—and he still does so with the Body and Blood of his own Son. From the first Passover in Egypt with the sacrifice of the unblemished lamb, to the manna sent down from the heavens to sustain the Israelites while they wandered through the desert, to King David's birth in Bethlehem, to the manger that held the newborn Son of God, to Jesus's teaching about himself as the bread come down from heaven, to the Last Supper: All of these point to Jesus's identity as the Bread of Life, the unblemished Lamb of God who takes away the sins of the world. He is food for our souls as well as for our bodies.

From the very beginning, God knew that he was going to let himself become small—so small, in fact, that he would become food for us to consume. He is both large enough for eternity and small enough to be digested. *Finally*, the intimacy we crave can be satisfied! The encounter with the Lord through the intimate setting of a shared meal can actually quiet our longings for something bigger than ourselves.

There is great promise in this gift, but it is also difficult to receive. A number of the first disciples left while Jesus was teaching us about his Real Presence, and this truth remains a challenge for many today. Even those of us who know and believe Jesus can robotically receive him in the Eucharist out of habit or routine. And yet, he remains faithful. Everything we have wanted all our lives, everything we have ever sought after, is given to us right then and there as we receive the Eucharist.

He fills us. And he has made it very clear that he wants intimacy with us more than anything—he died to make it possible! The Lord is ever faithful to his promises that he will be present to all who call upon him, and he will not fail to satisfy. His love and presence are worth more than anything in this world, if only we would come to him, ready to receive a taste of his light and life and love.

## TAKE TO PRAYER

- What needs do you have that you can turn over to the Lord?
- What remains unsatisfied in you? What do you truly long for? How can Jesus satisfy you?
- Imagine Jesus himself living inside of you. Ask him to help you carry his presence into the world today.

---

**PRAY WITH THIS LINE TODAY:**

You call me to your wedding banquet, and I run joyfully to you! Satisfy me, O Lord!

---

## DAY 13

# HOLY SPIRIT, YOU ARE WELCOME HERE!

---

### IF YOU ONLY HAVE TWO MINUTES TO PRAY TODAY, PRAY THIS:

Holy Spirit, move in me! Break in me everything that is not of you. I want more of you. Be present in me today, and guide my every step. Amen.

---

## RECEIVE FROM THE WORD

For those who are led by the Spirit of God are children of God. For you did not receive a spirit of slavery to fall back into fear, but you received a spirit of adoption, through which we cry, "Abba, Father!" The Spirit itself bears witness with our spirit that we are children of God, and if children, then heirs, heirs of God and joint heirs with Christ, if only we suffer with him so that we may also be glorified with him. (Rom 8:14–17)

## REFLECT

Did you know that you are a child of God?

Now pause right there. Throw out any previous conceptions you may have been given about being a "child of God" through a dusty religious education program. Most of the time when we hear this phrase, our minds immediately go to something nice and fluffy. Kumbaya won't cut it, though. So let's start again.

Did you know that God, the Creator and sustainer of the universe, the star-breather, the One who knows every human inside and out for all of eternity, has decided to *adopt* you into his family? Through baptism, you were fundamentally changed forever—you were given a new nature, a new self, a new identity.

You are now a daughter of God. The daughter of the King of the Universe isn't just loved. She has authority. She has responsibility. She is given gifts by the One who signed the adoption papers: the Holy Spirit. It is the Spirit who has changed you into an adopted daughter of God. And the Spirit longs to give you more gifts, more authority, more confidence in your identity. You just need to ask for it.

Let's take a look at Jesus's own baptism. We know that he did not *need* to be baptized, but his baptism was a model for us. At the moment of his baptism, the Holy Spirit descended upon him, and a voice came from heaven saying, "This is my beloved Son, with whom I am well pleased" (Mt 3:17). This is what happened to us at our own baptisms, imperceptible though it was. The Holy Spirit descended upon each of us, and the Lord spoke, "This is my beloved daughter, with whom I am well pleased."

God wants us to encounter the Holy Spirit anew in a life-transforming way. We experience the love of God the Father poured into our hearts by the Holy Spirit through a surrender to the Lordship of Jesus Christ. This encounter with the indwelling, creative life of the Trinity makes our identity as Christians come alive through our baptism and Confirmation. It deepens our relationship with God and others, gives us a zeal to bring God's love to others, and equips us with gifts for service. And who needs these resources more than mothers, who are tasked with raising our children and serving our families with God's love? It turns out that this powerful intimacy with the Holy Spirit was tailor-made to support the vocation of motherhood. The Spirit can give you everything you need to be a holy mom.

God is doing something in you right now! Perceptible or imperceptible, he's stirring up things within your soul to bring about life and newness. Holiness is something that God desires to do in *you*, within *your family*, not just in that other, holy-seeming mom who homeschools her twelve kids.

This is a call to heroic love, so we need all the help we can get! Yet, it can be hard to receive the gifts the Lord is offering us in this call. We've all been there: We go to Mass, say the words, separate kids so they'll stop touching their siblings, move the diaper bag so we can sit down, pull small children out from under the pew, stand, take the toddler out to go potty, kneel, and try to ignore the four-year-old giving mommy a new hair-do. Then we sleepily do it all again next week. Sometimes it feels as if Mass is nothing more than an impossible challenge of getting our kids to sit still for sixty minutes—but remember this: Regardless of our capacity to receive him, God is present to us. So we show up, trusting and believing that whatever scrap of attention we can offer the Lord will be taken up to the altar, prayed over, transformed, and given back to us as nourishment for this important work. Jesus makes himself available for us today, even if we're sleep-deprived, overwhelmed, or unsure of what day it is.

This indwelling of the Holy Spirit allows us to say, "Jesus is Lord"—and really mean it! It is what makes giving everything up for Jesus worth it. When we receive this encounter with the Holy Spirit, we experience Jesus in a real and profound way. Jesus is no longer merely someone we approach on Sundays; he is the sole focus of our lives. We participate in his love! And as we grow in relationship with the Spirit, our love and desire to share him with others grows. We are called to live radically in the Holy Spirit!

If you have never experienced the presence of the Holy Spirit, ask for it right now. From the first Pentecost until today, the Holy Spirit has always come in response to fervent and hungry prayer. Come, Holy Spirit!

## TAKE TO PRAYER

- How have you encountered the Holy Spirit moving in your life? Where did the Spirit lead you? How can you call on and trust the Spirit more?
- What would change about your life if you did everything under the influence of the Holy Spirit?
- What do you need from the Spirit right now?

---

**PRAY WITH THIS LINE TODAY:**

Fill me up, Lord, and overflow in me.

---

## DAY 14

# SUSTAINED BY YOUR PRESENCE

---

### IF YOU ONLY HAVE TWO MINUTES TO PRAY TODAY, PRAY THIS:

Lord Jesus, you are everything! You hold me and fashion me and sustain me. Give me life and peace by your presence today. Help me to see your movements in every moment. Amen.

---

## RECEIVE FROM THE WORD

When Jesus arrived, he found that Lazarus had already been in the tomb for four days. Now Bethany was near Jerusalem, only about two miles away. And many of the Jews had come to Martha and Mary to comfort them about their brother. When Martha heard that Jesus was coming, she went to meet him; but Mary sat at home. Martha said to Jesus, "Lord, if you had been here, my brother would not have died. [But] even now I know that whatever

> you ask of God, God will give you." Jesus said to her, "Your brother will rise." Martha said to him, "I know he will rise, in the resurrection on the last day." Jesus told her, "I am the resurrection and the life; whoever believes in me, even if he dies, will live, and everyone who lives and believes in me will never die. Do you believe this?" She said to him, "Yes, Lord. I have come to believe that you are the Messiah, the Son of God, the one who is coming into the world." (Jn 11:17–27)

## REFLECT

The Lord is here, and he is so close. Heaven seems so far away sometimes, and the daily grind does a great job of reminding us that we are not in heaven. And yet, every longing that we have for the presence of God is good. Every longing that we have for peace, for joy, for healing, or for love stems from this desire for heaven and the knowledge that we don't yet have it. But God did not give us this life to starve us of himself. When Jesus proclaims the kingdom of God, he doesn't say, "The kingdom will be great after you die, so just live your life and hang on!" He says that the kingdom is here, *now*.

God is found in the here and now. Yes, in heaven we will experience the perfection and fullness of his presence and love in the beatific vision. But God has gone to great lengths to make himself known throughout history. He is not a distant, cruel God who created the world as a lab experiment, taking notes a few paces away, just waiting to see what would happen. He is an immanent God. He is woven into the very fabric of existence itself. His presence sustains our lives; everything that we are exists because he is present in us. At every moment, we are on his mind. To leave the mind of God would be to cease to exist.

You are on God's mind right now. He sees you, notices you, and is pouring his love out upon you right now as you read these words.

Every time we recognize that we are in his presence, we discover a little bit more about what heaven might be like. The saints describe heaven as the ultimate experience of basking in the presence and love of God. Conversely, they describe hell as the absence of God. And the absence of God is torturous. But this makes sense, doesn't it? Even on earth, when we are close to the Lord and aware of his presence we do feel closer to heaven. We are filled with joy and peace and love and all those other happy words we might have plastered on a sign in our living rooms somewhere. And when we don't acknowledge God in our lives? When it's been a while since we've spoken to him, or sought his presence? Nothing in our lives seems to work quite right.

"Lord, if you had been here," cries Martha. *If you had been here.* The story of the raising of Lazarus and Jesus's conversation with Martha is a beautiful illustration of the power of the Lord's presence. Martha seems to have learned a few lessons since the last time we encountered her when she was distracted. She recognizes now that the presence of Jesus is literally life-giving. And the absence of his presence? It is death.

As the story continues, Jesus sees the tomb of Lazarus. At the sight of it, we read the shortest verse in the entire Bible: "And Jesus wept" (Jn 11:35). Why did Jesus weep, when he knew what he was about to do? Just a few verses before, Jesus gives hints to his disciples that he is going to allow Lazarus to die so that he can raise him. But the pain of loss is still real. Jesus feels the separation and grief that death brings.

This story ends miraculously: Jesus raises Lazarus from the dead. Though she couldn't imagine it, Martha believed in Jesus's power over life. She looked to the Lord in her grief and loss, and that faithfulness led to new life.

How can we emulate Martha's trust in the life that Jesus brings? When things go sideways in our families, how can we look to Jesus as she did? The Lord's presence is continually and freely offered to each of us every day, and it will sustain us if we choose to lean into it.

## TAKE TO PRAYER

- Consider the last week—when did you glimpse heaven in your family's life? When did the Lord seem near?
- How has the Lord shown he is desperate for you? How have you experienced him reaching for you?
- What are the ways that the Lord is sustaining your life?

---

**PRAY WITH THIS LINE TODAY:**

Sustain me in your presence,
Lord Jesus, and bring me life.

---

# WEEK 3: JOY

Social media platforms like Instagram and Pinterest can be a fun place to spend a little downtime—until they're not. Don't get me wrong, I love following creative accounts focused on DIYing your house or how to grow the maximum number of plants in a small garden bed. Catholic social media can be a mixed bag, filled with inspiring posts and beautiful art with a few misinterpretations of Church teaching scattered here and there by well-meaning influencers.

One of the major downsides of social media, however, is the comparison trap. We log on to escape or to get inspired and end up bereft of joy. And not just in superficial things, either. We can all relate to being jealous over someone's nice house or clothes. But what is *not* normal is being jealous over what the Lord is doing in someone else's life and *not mine*.

A major moment for me was during a recent SEEK conference. For those not familiar, SEEK is one of the biggest Catholic conferences in the country, run by FOCUS, whose mission is to form college students into disciples. Leading up to the SEEK conference one year, it felt as if every single one of my favorite Catholic speakers, musicians, podcasters, ministries, and businesses were there. Social media was constantly bombarding me with the message that "everyone is here but you." I felt as if I was missing out on the movement of God somehow. And that thought was stealing my joy.

What is joy? I think most of us inherently know that joy and happiness are not the same. But if that's the case, what's the difference? St. Francis of Assisi paints my favorite picture regarding joy. In teaching his fellow brothers about perfect joy, he describes a situation: Even if they converted every soul, and all the kings of Europe joined their community, and the brothers were given every supernatural gift, that still would not be reason for perfect joy. Instead, St. Francis asks his friars to imagine a different scene. He has them picture himself traveling on a long journey in the deep of winter. It is the dead of night, and he is weary. He has icicles on his habit, his legs are bleeding, and he is covered in mud and snow, starving and freezing. After arriving at the door to their monastery and knocking for a long time, his fellow brothers do not recognize him and instead decide to drag him by his hood and beat him in the snow. Francis says, "If I am able to bear all this for love of God, not only with patience but with happiness, convinced that I deserve no other treatment, know, remember, and write down on your paper, God's little sheep, that at last I have found perfect joy."

Joy comes with bearing all things, knowing and basking in the fact that the Lord is near. He is immanent, and we have nothing to fear, nothing to dread! In other words, joy is not at all contingent upon our outside circumstances; rather, it is completely and totally reliant on the Lord and our assurance of his love and presence in our lives. Imagine the freedom that we would experience with true joy! Nothing—truly, nothing—could take it away! Not when the toddler is having a meltdown. Not when our kids are complaining about dinner. Not when our teen earns a less-than-stellar score on his SAT.

This means that true joy can be cultivated through intimacy with the Lord. We can't choose to feel happy, but we can choose to welcome God into our lives—especially because he's already here, waiting to be noticed! We don't need to wait for good things to happen in our lives until we "stumble" upon them. Joy is truly a fruit of the Holy Spirit. When we have the Holy Spirit moving and working in our lives, joy comes with it.

Back to the SEEK conference. In my own wallowing and sadness of "missing out" on God's movement, I heard the Lord say this to me for all the other moms who felt this way:

> Dear moms: I know it can be hard to see all the posts of your favorite brands, influencers, and speakers at SEEK right now. It is clear I am doing something there. But I need you to know that you are *not* missing out on the movement of God. You are exactly where you need to be for the salvation of your soul. If SEEK were necessary for your salvation, I would have made it so that you would be there. Lean in where you are meant to be *now*. I come down the mountain to visit you in your homes, in your dishes and laundry, in your cold cup of coffee, in the mismatched socks, and in the laughter of your children. Don't disparage this stage of life. Rejoice in the fact that I bring you to where you are, and I will not leave you alone.

Joy can be found in your home—yes, even in *your* home. Even in your heart. Despite your outside circumstances, or where your mind tends to wander, his peace, his love, and his joy can all be found here, in the midst of your vocation. Lean into the Lord, and you will find true joy. Choose him when it is difficult, bask in his love when it is easy, and let his love consume you!

## TAKE TO PRAYER

- Spend a minute telling the Lord that you wish to find joy in your current vocation and circumstances.
- Ask him to lead you to find that joy during the retreat this week.

## WATCH AND LISTEN

To watch a video introduction to this week, scan the QR code or visit www.avemariapress.com/pages/sacred-chaos-resources. You'll also find there a playlist with music to accompany your daily prayer.

# DAY 15

# SURRENDER IN THE STORM

---

### IF YOU ONLY HAVE TWO MINUTES TO PRAY TODAY, PRAY THIS:

I surrender to you, Lord. When the waves around me crash, and the storm is impossible to see through, let me be totally at peace with true joy in my heart, knowing you are here. You love me. And I delight in your love. Amen.

---

## RECEIVE FROM THE WORD

On that day, as evening drew on, Jesus said to them, "Let us cross to the other side." Leaving the crowd, they took him with them in the boat just as he was. And other boats were with him. A violent squall came up and waves were breaking over the boat, so that it was already filling up. Jesus was in the stern, asleep on a cushion. They woke him and said to him, "Teacher, do you not care that we are perishing?" He woke up, rebuked the wind, and said to the sea, "Quiet! Be still!" The wind ceased and there was great

> calm. Then he asked them, "Why are you terrified? Do you not yet have faith?" They were filled with great awe and said to one another, "Who then is this whom even wind and sea obey?" (Mk 4:35–41)

## REFLECT

The fact that motherhood comes with many jobs is not news to any of us. We all knew that we would be kissing boo-boos, having heart-to-hearts, organizing toys, and managing meltdowns. What might have come as a surprise is the mental load: keeping track of school emails, balancing the calendar, organizing the birthday parties, and making sure our kids get to where they need to be on time.

If we're not careful, the mental load can totally consume us. I often find myself so overwhelmed with to-dos that I freeze, unable to move forward to complete the smallest task. My mind becomes a storm, swirling with thoughts, tossing me around until I am afraid I'm going to drown in the waves. But where is Jesus in all this?

Our faith tells us that Jesus is already on the boat, my friends. He is bigger than the to-do list. It's when we begin to drown in our own thoughts and cry out, "Lord, help me!" that Jesus stands up. As we see in this story, he doesn't teach us how to sail the boat through the storm. He doesn't point to a safer harbor to wait it out. With all power and authority given to him, he commands the storm and our thoughts, "Quiet! Be still!" Peace. He brings *peace.*

The swirling, storming thoughts clamor for my attention, but don't need to have a claim on my heart. Yes, there is the to-do list. But that list is not my commander. That list is not my lord. There is only one who has permission to take my mind and heart, and his name is Jesus Christ. This act of surrendering to Christ is a daily choice we must make, sometimes moment to moment.

Peace. Be still. The Lord of heaven and earth is near—he is with us in this storm. There is such peace in knowing that we are loved more than we could ever desire. Even when our hearts wander, his love draws us back. We enter into this true joy when, despite our circumstances, we can rejoice in the peace and presence of Christ given to us. He is here, within our boats. And he says, "Peace. Be still."

## TAKE TO PRAYER

- Close your eyes and imagine the storms blowing in your life at this moment. Feel the stressors as if they were wind, rain, and waves battering you. Then turn to Jesus. What does he say?
- What do you think of when you hear the word *surrender*? What needs to be surrendered in your life?
- What is peace? How would your life change if you had it?

---

**PRAY WITH THIS LINE TODAY:**

Lord, give me peace amid the storms.

---

## DAY 16

# ARMS WIDE OPEN

---

### IF YOU ONLY HAVE TWO MINUTES TO PRAY TODAY, PRAY THIS:

Lord, your mercy knows no bounds!
Thank you, Lord, for the constant love
you shower over me and my family.
Even when I fall, there you are waiting,
with arms wide open. Amen.

---

## RECEIVE FROM THE WORD

For as the heavens tower over the earth,
    so his mercy towers over those who fear him.
As far as the east is from the west,
    so far has he removed our sins from us.
As a father has compassion on his children,
    so the LORD has compassion on those who fear him.
For he knows how we are formed,
    remembers that we are dust.

As for man, his days are like the grass;
he blossoms like a flower in the field.
A wind sweeps over it and it is gone;
its place knows it no more.
But the LORD's mercy is from age to age,
toward those who fear him.
His salvation is for the children's children
of those who keep his covenant,
and remember to carry out his precepts.
(Ps 103:11–18)

## REFLECT

Jesus has saved us and redeemed us! Even when we fall, he is there with arms outstretched, waiting for us. He knows our failings better than we do, and yet he runs to meet us to bring us into his loving embrace. He sacrificed his life on the Cross, enduring the worst pain we could inflict upon him, all to prove to us the depth of his love.

Jesus gives hints to his disciples that he will suffer and die before it even happens when he shares the parable of the prodigal son. Most of us know the story, but I invite you to journey a little deeper into this picture of the love of the Father. In this story, the younger son requests that his father give him his inheritance now—in other words, he asks for what he is to inherit once his father is dead. He doesn't say the words "I can't wait for you to die"—but his actions speak them.

But then, as Jesus tells the story, he says something interesting: "After a few days, the younger son collected all his belongings and set off to a distant country where he squandered his inheritance on a life of dissipation" (Lk 15:13). Notice that first phrase: "After a few days." This means the younger son asked for his inheritance, received it, and then didn't leave immediately. He waited a few days.

What was the interaction between the father and the younger son like in those few days? Surely the father knew exactly what the son was going to do. Maybe he tried to convince him to stay. Maybe he tried to bargain with him or plead with him. It's almost certain that the younger son felt nothing but contempt and disdain for the father, knowing that what he was about to do was wrong, but planning to do it anyway.

If I were the father in this story, I would probably put up a big fight—I'd tell my son all the reasons he was wrong, all the reasons he would be ruining his future and his family. I would tell him that I didn't raise him this way. I would tell him that the life he was about to choose would have no meaning. And when he would ultimately leave, I would feel bitter and angry. Part of me might even want to yell, "Good riddance!" or "Don't come back crying to me!"

But that doesn't happen. The son squanders his wealth and is left hiring himself out to work with the pigs, the most unclean of animals for the Jews. The son becomes desperate—desperate enough to decide to return home and beg his father to let him become a hired hand. Rehearsing what he wants to say in his mind, he thinks, "I shall get up and go to my father, and I shall say to him, 'Father, I have sinned against heaven and against you. I no longer deserve to be called your son; treat me as you would treat one of your hired workers'" (Lk 15:18–19).

But his plan never comes to fruition. As it turns out, the father is out, keeping an eye on the horizon, waiting, hoping, watching for his son to return. While the son is still a long way off, the father catches sight of him and runs to him. The son tries to get his rehearsed line out, but never gets a chance to finish. The father's arms are wide open, ready to receive him, not as a slave, but as a son. The son barely gets a chance to repent, and the father already knows exactly what he is going to do to celebrate his son who has returned.

This is what the Lord does to us. He knows how much we can hurt him. He knows what we struggle with and the excuses we tell ourselves before we even make a decision. And yet, he knows exactly how to celebrate our return. He knows how badly we want to be redeemed and made whole and forgiven.

Have you ever considered that the Lord wants to redeem you more than you want to be redeemed yourself? That he will go to great lengths to pull you into his loving embrace?

Before the words even come out of our mouths, he is running to us, with arms wide open! As we walk back toward the Father, he has caught sight of us and runs as fast as he can to catch up and meet us where we are. We are truly loved, truly redeemed, truly caught up in the loving embrace of God.

## TAKE TO PRAYER

- What does God want to redeem in you?
- What sins do you have a hard time forgiving yourself for? What does the Lord say to you about them?
- Imagine that the Lord has his arms open to you. How do you respond?

---

**PRAY WITH THIS LINE TODAY:**

Let me run into your open arms.

---

## DAY 17

# LIVING IN THE OVERFLOW

### IF YOU ONLY HAVE TWO MINUTES TO PRAY TODAY, PRAY THIS:

Lord, you are living inside of me!
At every moment, you care for me.
Be my shepherd today. Guide me
to green pastures, Jesus. Amen.

## RECEIVE FROM THE WORD

So Jesus said again, "Amen, amen, I say to you, I am the gate for the sheep. All who came [before me] are thieves and robbers, but the sheep did not listen to them. I am the gate. Whoever enters through me will be saved, and will come in and go out and find pasture. A thief comes only to steal and slaughter and destroy; I came so that they might have life and have it more abundantly. I am the good shepherd. A good shepherd lays down his life for the sheep. A hired man, who is not a shepherd and whose sheep are not his own, sees a wolf coming and leaves the

> sheep and runs away, and the wolf catches and scatters them. This is because he works for pay and has no concern for the sheep. I am the good shepherd, and I know mine and mine know me, just as the Father knows me and I know the Father; and I will lay down my life for the sheep." (Jn 10:7–15)

## REFLECT

Why are we tempted to believe that God only wants to give us bits and pieces of himself? Why are we tempted to believe that God will only give us the amount we need to survive? It's just not true! The Lord wants to overflow in our hearts. Yes, he wants to give us what we need. But he also wants to give us an abundance of himself, not make himself scarce. He would never have become man to die on the Cross if he were planning to lead his sheep only to patches of pasture. He would never give himself in the Eucharist if he were not planning to find the greenest pasture around and lead us to it.

It's time to stop believing that God doesn't want what is *best* for us and our families. He is not only protecting us from the thief that comes to steal, kill, and destroy, but he has promised us life! And not just any life—*abundant* life! An abundant life for our families, for our marriages, for our kids, for the inner workings of our souls. He doesn't just fill us—he desires for us to live in the overflow of his presence, so much so that it spills out into everyone we meet, everyone we come into contact with. He wants his presence to overflow in our lives in such abundance that it touches our kids, so they can feel the presence of God in our homes, within us, and within themselves, as they get to know the Lord as they grow.

The Lord intends to overflow in our lives in such a great capacity that we may never even know how many people he touches. Consider the story of the feeding of the five thousand in Matthew 14. Jesus is weary and needs some quiet and rest. That need is not met, however, when he is faced with thousands of people who have left their homes to follow him into the deserted place that he picked for himself. Moved with pity, he cures the sick they have brought him. It's getting late at this point, with thousands of people everywhere and not a single Panera in sight. Of course, no one thought to pack a lunch; they heard Jesus was heading to a deserted place, so they dropped everything to follow him. Well, except for one person, that is.

One boy, sent with five loaves and two fish, was smart enough to bring a snack. The rest of the story is pretty familiar: Jesus takes the loaves and fish, blesses them, breaks them, and tells the disciples to pass them out. Five thousand men, not counting women and children, were totally fed off the loaves and fish, with twelve baskets full left over. Not too shabby for an intended day off.

But have we ever stopped to think: Who packed the boy's lunch? Who baked the bread? Who kneaded it or let it rise? Imagine with me the boy's mother, working hard to keep her family fed, cared for, and out of trouble. See her measuring grain, letting it rise for just the right amount of time, and baking it so that it would be ready for her son to eat. I can imagine the boy running into the house, calling out, "The teacher! He is not far! Mother, I'm going to follow him!" And his mother frantically calls out, "Wait a moment! Take this just in case. You know how hungry you get in the sun." I see his mother grabbing a cloth and quickly stuffing a few quick loaves that were fresh from the oven and wrapping them hurriedly so that her son would not leave without them. Remembering, too, that there are some fish that need to be eaten before they go bad, she grabs a couple and puts them with the bread. "Take this!" she calls out as her son grabs the food and runs to see the teacher.

Did this mother have any idea what miracle would be done with her labor? Did she have any idea how many people would be fed by the bread she made? The hidden work of measuring grain, kneading dough, and baking the bread turned into a bounty in the Lord's hands. Jesus used her gifts, her love, her work, her simple vocation. He took them, small as they were, and put his presence into them. And he fashioned one of the most famous miracles that he ever performed out of them. The overflow of himself through her is still inspiring us two thousand years later.

I also imagine this mother sitting in her kitchen after hearing the story of what happened with the bread she made—fingering the flour she used; touching the table she kneaded the bread on; sitting, basking, knowing that God was with her as she made that bread that would feed so many. Maybe it dawns on her that the miracle may very well have been the turning point for someone in their realization that Jesus is God. Perhaps she ponders how the Lord used her work to satisfy not only the stomachs of many but their souls as well. She's basking in the overflow of grace that God poured out through her house, her hands, her love.

God wants to pour out his presence in your soul too. He wants to show you that he has come to give you life and to give it in abundance.

## TAKE TO PRAYER

- How has the Lord been pouring himself out in abundance in your life?
- What parts of your daily labor can you put into the Lord's hands? Where have you noticed an overflow of his presence?
- What "green pastures" is God leading you to?

---

### PRAY WITH THIS LINE TODAY:

You came that I might have life;
draw me into your abundance.

---

## DAY 18

# THE RESOUNDING WORD

---

**IF YOU ONLY HAVE TWO MINUTES TO PRAY TODAY, PRAY THIS:**

Teach me to sit with your Word, O Lord.
Speak to me in every action and
movement I make today. Amen.

---

## RECEIVE FROM THE WORD

In the beginning was the Word,
  and the Word was with God,
  and the Word was God.
He was in the beginning with God.
All things came to be through him,
  and without him nothing came to be.
What came to be through him was life,
  and this life was the light of the human race;
the light shines in the darkness,
  and the darkness has not overcome it.
(Jn 1:1–5)

# REFLECT

Wouldn't it be great if the Lord would place a big sign in the sky to tell us what he wants? Or if he would make it clear and obvious that he's real through some miraculous gesture?

The reality is that the Lord has already revealed himself to us in the most radical way: He became one of us. The Word became flesh. And why is Jesus, the second person of the Trinity, referred to as the Word? He is God himself, speaking his creative love out over all of creation and existence for all eternity. The Son could have been described as "the Presence" or some other passive phrase. But he isn't—he is the Word, who is active, constantly moving, constantly reverberating, constantly reaching out. "The Word," or *Logos* in Greek, literally means "expression." Jesus is the expression of God himself. And it makes sense: That's what a word does—it communicates.

Jesus's expression of God can be seen clearly in a famous encounter. He was approached one day by a man desperately needing his help. It was a situation so dire that time was not on their side. Of course, nothing Jesus did in public was a simple affair. Crowds of people with desperate situations, hungry hearts, and burning questions pushed one another out of the way, trying to get a glimpse or a word in with the Master. The man who had approached Jesus tried to move as many people as he could out of the way. The sun beat down, and sweat dripped from Jesus's brow as he breathed in the smell of a growing crowd of hot, unwashed people, continually hindering his progress toward his destination.

At the same time, a woman, driven by desperation and a burst of audacity, felt a surge of hope coursing through her body. *No*, she thought—*I can't.* "Why not?" a voice in her heart asked. Unsure of the source of boldness and definite impertinence, she yielded to the call in her heart before she had a chance to change her mind. No one was looking at her; they were all looking at him. She got as close as she dared on her feet, unsure of how to get close enough. "Keep going," the voice urged. The woman pushed through the crowd and ducked as low as she could, aware of the Jewish laws she was breaking by touching the people in the crowd as an unclean woman, but magnetically drawn to the voice she had felt.

He was close but being pushed away faster and faster. There was no way she would be able to speak with him. *If I could but touch him*, she thought. This was her one chance. *Now.* She threw her body as hard as she could and grabbed on to his garment. Immediately, the power of the Word of God coursed through her body. God's healing love was communicated to her in that instant, more deeply and more intimately than the mere words of any person, let alone any doctor she had seen for her affliction. Her constant flow of blood immediately dried up, and she was healed.

Jesus—this resounding, holy Echo—speaks to us constantly, even when we assume he's silent. Even when we're not aware of his words, they are there. Even when we are distracted or overwhelmed, or when we think he's saying nothing at all, he speaks love over our lives. Existence itself is spoken over our lives. He needs nothing else except himself to bring forth life, which means that we need nothing else other than the presence of this Word. And there is nothing in our lives that is too insignificant to be spoken of by the Word. He speaks every moment of joy that we experience with a massive exclamation point. He speaks every moment of sorrow gently, sweetly. And we are invited to cling to his words as if they are the very foundation of life itself. Because as it turns out, they are.

In every word that he speaks to me, there is one resounding Word that he speaks over me: *love, love, love*. He is the Word of the Father, who is Love itself—the fullness of his revelation to the world. When I don't know what God wants to say to me, when I seek his voice, I simply turn to the one Word that he forever speaks to my heart: *Jesus, Jesus, Jesus.*

## TAKE TO PRAYER

- Quiet your mind and heart. What is Jesus—God's Word—saying to you right here in this moment?
- How have you encountered the Word in your life? Where have you heard the echo of God's Word resounding?
- Recall a time when Jesus felt distant, and ask the Lord what he was speaking over you in that moment.

---

**PRAY WITH THIS LINE TODAY:**

Speak, Lord; your servant is listening.

---

## DAY 19

# SAFE IN YOUR GAZE

---

### IF YOU ONLY HAVE TWO MINUTES TO PRAY TODAY, PRAY THIS:

I am safe with you, Lord. You guide me on my path and lead me where you want me to go. Transform me. Restore me. Satisfy me, Lord. Help me rest in your gaze today. Amen.

---

## RECEIVE FROM THE WORD

The LORD is my shepherd;
there is nothing I lack.
In green pastures he makes me lie down;
to still waters he leads me;
he restores my soul.
He guides me along right paths
for the sake of his name.

Even though I walk through the valley of the shadow of
death,
I will fear no evil, for you are with me;
your rod and your staff comfort me.

You set a table before me
in front of my enemies;
You anoint my head with oil;
my cup overflows.
Indeed, goodness and mercy will pursue me
all the days of my life;
I will dwell in the house of the LORD
for endless days.
(Ps 23)

## REFLECT

It's hard not to focus on the phrase "valley of the shadow of death" when we read Psalm 23. Out of all the metaphors King David uses as he writes this psalm, this one is the most arresting. There certainly are days when the bathroom floor feels like the valley of the shadow of death.

But as mothers, let's see if there might be some good news to find in this psalm. What about this line: "He makes me lie down"? Or this one: "To still waters he leads me; he restores my soul"? Or this: "There is nothing I lack"? Boy, I don't know any better phrases that sum up the desires of motherhood. When is the last time I lay down? When is the last time I felt as if my life was like still water, as opposed to a rush of rapids or a tsunami? And I almost laugh at the phrase "there is nothing I lack"—what a nice fairytale that would be.

And yet, what is the Lord saying to us here through this psalm? He's telling us to rest, commanding us to rest. "See this pasture right here?" he says. "See this place I've led you to? You can lie down here. It's time. You can stop striving and seeking and working. Here, in my gaze, you can rest. It's okay that there is laundry to do. It's okay that there are emails with your name on it. Those can wait. The pasture is green, and the grass is good. Eat your fill! See this water that I've led you to? It's safe to drink. You aren't going to get frightened by a crocodile or a piranha jumping up out of the water to bite you in the nose the moment things get good."

Because that's the temptation, isn't it? The moment things start to get good, we become tempted to think that any second the other shoe is going to drop, and God is going to take something away from us. The defecation is going to hit the oscillation, and I need to take cover and brace myself.

But God does not want us to live like that! He wants us to know that we are truly safe in his gaze. Lie down in his pastures, and drink the still water. Let him restore you and satisfy you. Yes, there will be times when the Lord will allow you to tread through the valley of the shadow of death. But your time there is meant to be spent in total reliance on him, who is with you every step of the way. In total peace—comforted, even. That doesn't seem so bad, does it?

Even when the lions and wolves and other predators come looking for some lost-looking sheep, remember this: The sheep who are the most in danger are the ones who do not trust the shepherd. The shepherd's rod and staff are there to guide and lead us to where we need to go—and, if necessary, to beat down a hungry wolf. But when we sense danger, temptation, anxiety, or events that happen in our lives that shake us, we have a tendency to freeze or even ignore the shepherd who is calling us to come to him for protection. We can't always see the whole picture—but God does. When he calls, we need to respond. His call comes with a certain degree of freedom and joy that we could never have on our own. Relying on the Good Shepherd and the way he prepares for us gives us the freedom to choose what is good and turn from what is not. And we can have joy in knowing that we are protected in him.

Whether you're at the green pastures, on your way there, or walking through the valley, draw near to the Lord—he will fill you with joy. He continually calls us to him, and knowing that we are safe here in his gaze brings peace to our souls.

## TAKE TO PRAYER

- Where is the Lord leading you today? Imagine the type of terrain he has brought you to.
- What dangers is the Lord protecting you from? What are the green pastures you seek?
- What does the phrase "he restores my soul" mean to you? What parts of your soul need restoring?

---

**PRAY WITH THIS LINE TODAY:**

Help me to find rest in you, Lord.

---

## DAY 20

# FREEDOM IN THE SPIRIT

---

### IF YOU ONLY HAVE TWO MINUTES TO PRAY TODAY, PRAY THIS:

Come, Holy Spirit! Give me the freedom that comes with living in your glory. Whatever gifts and grace you want to give me, I ask that you help me receive them. I come to you freely with open arms. Come, Holy Spirit. Amen.

---

## RECEIVE FROM THE WORD

Therefore, since we have such hope, we act very boldly and not like Moses, who put a veil over his face so that the Israelites could not look intently at the cessation of what was fading. Rather, their thoughts were rendered dull, for to this present day the same veil remains unlifted when they read the old covenant, because through Christ it is taken away. To this day, in fact, whenever Moses is read, a veil lies over their hearts, but whenever a person turns to the Lord the veil is removed. Now the Lord is the Spirit,

> and where the Spirit of the Lord is, there is freedom. All of us, gazing with unveiled face on the glory of the Lord, are being transformed into the same image from glory to glory, as from the Lord who is the Spirit. (2 Cor 3:12–18)

## REFLECT

The gospels give us such a colorful picture of the different people Jesus interacted with: Nicodemus, Mary and Martha, the healed leper, the woman at the well, Mary Magdalene, Zacchaeus, and the various apostles are just a few of the characters we get to know while reading the New Testament. But one limitation we have unconsciously embraced is to confine them to their own stories, as if they never interacted with one another or were present for any other event besides the ones they are named in. The sending of the Holy Spirit at Pentecost was a major event in the communities that Jesus walked in and touched many of the people we hear about in the gospels.

I have to wonder: How did the lives of each of these individuals change once Pentecost happened? How did their lives change when they received the Holy Spirit in power? We get a good glimpse at what happens to Peter: He goes from someone who is hotheaded and temperamental with something to prove (and often can't back it up) to someone who is articulate, convincing, and fearless. People will sit and wait in the hopes that his shadow will pass over them. Peter, who once lied to a group of lowly servants to save his own hide, now openly proclaims Jesus resurrected and actually looks for opportunities to pray for healing over people who are crippled. He now confronts the high priests, tells them that if the choice is between obeying them or God, they can go pound sand. And when faced with prison, he continues preaching with all boldness despite the very real threat to his life.

The descent of the Holy Spirit changes everything—everything! We are no longer bound by the limitations we've placed on ourselves, or that others have placed on us. The Holy Spirit now gives us the freedom to live according to the love of God. Check out what happens in Acts 3. Peter and John are headed to the Temple to pray and see a man crippled from birth begging for alms. Most of us would either offer a quick prayer for the man, maybe give him a dollar, or avoid his gaze all together. But not Peter. Set free by the Holy Spirit to do exactly what God has placed on his heart, Peter prays for healing over the man. And the man is actually healed!

I wonder how the lives of the other characters in the New Testament changed. Perhaps Martha, once concerned about having everything "just so," was set free to love by the Holy Spirit. Maybe Zacchaeus, the converted tax collector, was set on fire with the presence of the Spirit. Even Nicodemus—I wonder what happened to him? If he received the Holy Spirit, how did it change his life, which was full of wondering and sincere questions? Unfortunately, we may not know the answers to those questions until we meet these people in heaven. But there is one "before and after" transformation that we *are* privileged to witness from a front-row seat: our own.

Where the Spirit of the Lord is, there is freedom! With the Lord, we can do all things! His Spirit enables us to love like we've never loved before. To move and work and pray with "power and love and self-control" (2 Tm 1:7). The Spirit gives us the words to say when we don't know what to say. In our weakness, the Holy Spirit is our strength. We have nothing to fear, for the Spirit of the Lord is with us. Where the Spirit of the Lord is, there is freedom!

## TAKE TO PRAYER

- What parts of your life need to be transformed by the Holy Spirit?
- In what ways do you not feel free? If the Lord is leading you to find more freedom by depending on him, how can you turn to him in moments of need?
- Talk to the Holy Spirit about how you want him to transform your life. Having articulated your wants, which desires resonate

as being inspired by God and which feel more shallow? How can you better stay in touch with God's voice and what the Spirit wants for you?

---

### PRAY WITH THIS LINE TODAY:

Come, Holy Spirit, and lead me to freedom.

---

## DAY 21

# EVERYTHING FOR YOUR GLORY!

---

### IF YOU ONLY HAVE TWO MINUTES TO PRAY TODAY, PRAY THIS:

All glory be to the Father, and to the Son, and to the Holy Spirit. As it was in the beginning, is now, and ever shall be, world without end. Amen.

---

## RECEIVE FROM THE WORD

Shout joyfully to God, all the earth;
    sing of his glorious name;
    give him glorious praise.
Say to God: "How awesome your deeds!
    Before your great strength your enemies cringe.
All the earth falls in worship before you;
    they sing of you, sing of your name!"
*Selah*

Come and see the works of God,
  awesome in deeds before the children of Adam.
He changed the sea to dry land;
  through the river they passed on foot.
There we rejoiced in him,
  who rules by his might forever,
His eyes are fixed upon the nations.
  Let no rebel rise to challenge!
*Selah*
Bless our God, you peoples;
  loudly sound his praise,
Who has kept us alive
  and not allowed our feet to slip.
(Ps 66:2–9)

## REFLECT

What do you think of when you think of the glory of God? I often picture a mountain, covered in storm clouds with lightning and thunder crashing around it. I can see the shadows that the clouds make on the desert surrounding it, and the Lord of Glory takes creation in his hands and molds it and shapes it however he chooses. The book of Revelation also shows us many examples of God's glory, featuring angels and trumpets and creatures bowing low to the Lamb who was slain. He defeats his enemies with one hand—and with the other, he rescues me.

But it's not just on mountains or the battlefield where God's glory shines—our lives are supposed to be a reflection of his glory too. How is this possible for an everyday mother? I'm just a mom. I take kids to school and dry tears and wipe butts and convince my kids that "Mommy doesn't make yucky food." How does this life that I lead reflect the glory of God? Nothing that I do in my daily life is as awe-inspiring as a mountain covered in a thunderstorm. Right?

As I write these words, I feel a wave of movement near my stomach area. My unborn baby kicks my belly, rolls around, and then checks to make sure my bladder is good and empty. Thankfully, it is. New life is living and growing inside of me: someone with a soul, a future, an identity—a human person who will have the capacity to choose and to love and to reflect God back to the rest of humanity. Someone created in God's image and likeness, destined for heaven and, you guessed it, glory.

How could someone as insignificant as myself reflect back God's glory? We pray, "All is for your glory, Lord," and "We give you glory," but how could we even begin to "contribute" to God's glory? For this question, let's call in the professional: Mama Mary. She knows what it's like to be insignificant. She knows what it's like to be hidden and inconsequential. And she, better than any human in history, knows what it means to give her life to God's glory. Not only does she give her whole life to glorify God, but she also knows what it means to be caught up in that glory herself. In her famous hymn of praise, the Magnificat, she prays:

> My soul proclaims the greatness of the Lord;
> my spirit rejoices in God my savior.
> For he has looked upon his handmaid's lowliness;
> behold, from now on will all ages call me blessed.
> The Mighty One has done great things for me,
> and holy is his name.
> His mercy is from age to age
> to those who fear him.
> He has shown might with his arm,
> dispersed the arrogant of mind and heart.
> He has thrown down the rulers from their thrones
> but lifted up the lowly.
> The hungry he has filled with good things;
> the rich he has sent away empty.
> He has helped Israel his servant,
> remembering his mercy,
> according to his promise to our fathers,
> to Abraham and to his descendants forever.
> (Lk 1:46–55)

It is in Mary's motherhood that she experiences glory and gives God glory. In her quiet existence as a young mother to a small kid, she is experiencing something so much more significant than some old thunderstorm up on a mountaintop. And do you remember what brought her here to begin with? It was her *fiat*—her yes to God's plan for her life. In her obedience, she unties the strangling disobedience of Eve and finds God's glory in the life he has planned for her.

It's the same for us, isn't it? We aren't called to be the mother of the Son of God. We each have a totally different trajectory of life than Mary. We all have different temperaments, gifts, and homes to tend. But God still intends to offer each of us the path that he created us for.

You still have the opportunity to say yes to whatever that path is. God still intends to use you for his glory.

## TAKE TO PRAYER

- What do you think of when you think of the glory of God—how do you picture it?
- How do you give God glory in your daily life? How is he calling you to give him glory?
- What parts of your life might already be shining forth with God's glory in ways that are reflected in Mary's Magnificat?

---

**PRAY WITH THIS LINE TODAY:**

Let everything I do be done for your glory!

---

# CONCLUSION

This twenty-one-day journey that we have embarked upon is not meant to simply end. We have been through too much with the Lord, being molded and shaped to be more like him, to simply stop pursuing him. We have experienced desire and lack of desire. We have encountered the Lord in different ways. We have chosen joy and leaned into the peace he brings us. Now is the time to begin to implement a regular habit of daily prayer so that we can continue to walk with the Lord through our family life. We know what it means to not want to pray and to choose it anyway. We can lean on that experience for the coming times in our lives when we will encounter dryness and distraction.

So many of us have felt discouraged in prayer as mothers. We may have even been told that growing deeper in prayer is going to have to wait until our kids are out of the house. But as we have experienced over the last twenty-one days, it is just not true that we have to wait for a better time to attend to our faith. God made motherhood knowing how difficult it would be. He did not intend for us to have an entire period of our lives where he is absent. Desiring the Lord is *for* mothers. Encountering him is *for* mothers. Living in his joy and peace is *for* mothers. We need the Lord now. We need him now more than we ever have needed him before in our lives. And he does not intend to leave that need unmet.

My hope is that after completing this book, you will have formed enough of a habit of daily prayer to continue walking in the Spirit. But what to do? My favorite way to pray is by reading scripture. If reading the Bible is new for you, start with the gospels: Matthew, Mark, Luke, and John, which are located in the last third of the Bible. Or visit the website for the United States Conference of Catholic Bishops (usccb .org) to read the gospel passage that is used for daily Mass. Read a story, close your eyes, and imagine yourself in the scene with Jesus. Pay attention to what the Lord is saying to you. What is he drawing your attention to? Ask him about it.

Another great way to continue to practice daily prayer is to journal. You can write down anything you want to say to God. Be honest and open, and you may find that the Lord speaks to you through the very words that you are writing as you write them. There are a number of prayer journals available (including *The Ave Prayer Intentions Journal*, which structures prayer encounters according to your needs), but all you really need is a blank page.

I pray that through this twenty-one-day journey, you have encountered the Lord speaking to you in a new way. I pray that you have discovered or rediscovered an intimacy with him that will continue to grow and flourish throughout your motherhood journey, as well as through the rest of your life. Everything we do to seek the Lord is ultimately a movement of God himself, urging us to seek him and find him. And you will indeed find him, if you are seeking with all your heart.

## CLOSING PRAYER

Take my life, Lord, and make it yours! In my motherhood, in my life, let every decision I make be saturated with your Spirit. Lead me where you want me to go. Give me wisdom and discernment in how to raise my children. Give me humility in my marriage. Speak to me, Lord, for I am listening. Speak your Word through me to the people you have put in my life. I ask this through your Son, our Lord Jesus Christ, and the intercession of his mother and ours, Mary.

# ACKNOWLEDGMENTS

How can I start this acknowledgments page without sounding as if I'm bragging about how many people I have in my life? The Lord decided he wanted this book written, and he moved all the pieces and people to make it happen. I thank these people not only for this book but for coming into my life and making it so good.

Special thanks go to all the women of the Prayer Intentions Signal group, who prayed for me and encouraged me when I felt defeated. Special shout-outs to Paula Golbabi, Jenny White, Becka Gerhart, Sarah Adams, Teresa Kohnert, Rachel Koucmoud, and all the women of the St. Thomas children's adoration crowd who gave me their feedback on what they needed in prayer. Thank you to Alyssa Trutter, Emily Shimek, Samantha Shephard, Amanda Kapchinski, Britt Erisman, Stephanie Lafitte, Carolyn Baudoin, Brittany Taunton, Ashley McCullough, Claire Ting, Amanda Naeger, and Chris Bartlett for their longtime support of this book and of me. Thank you for encouraging me and warding away imposter syndrome. Thank you to Tammy and Whitney Marbach for the ideas you shared. Thank you to my mom, Sylvia Masters, for paving the way and giving me a view of what committed daily prayer looks like. Thanks to Sarah Sullivan and Regina Gray for praying through this book with me, and to Matt Sullivan for the idea. Shout-out to Taylor Schroll for connecting me with Kathryn, and to Kathryn Whitacre for the introductions. I am incredibly grateful to Heidi Hess Saxton for her belief in me as a writer and for advocating for me. This book would not exist without her.

Thank you to my in-laws, Delbert and Veronica Stavinoha, for taking the kids for a few days so that I could write. And thank you to my husband Jeremy, for his complete support of me and of this process. Thank you for giving me the space to write, for encouraging me to keep going, and for your belief in me. Thank you for praying for me in your truly unreal discipline in prayer, while I struggle with mine. Thanks for never giving up on me.

Lastly and most importantly, thank you, Lord, for everything. Thank you for your faithfulness and your goodness. You know my heart, and it is full of gratitude.

# APPENDIX: 4-WEEK GUIDE FOR SMALL GROUPS

This guide will help you gather with other mothers over four weeks to open your hearts to the Lord and to one another. Over the course of these gatherings, you will meet other women who are also searching for holiness through their experiences of motherhood—together, you'll find strength, support, and inspiration to become more like the saints we are called to be. This format offers a structure for weekly meetings that could easily be carried out over Zoom if childcare is a challenge, or even at a playground as the kids scamper around the jungle gym.

This small group might become the foundation for a new or deeper experience of community, but even if you don't continue to gather together, you can trust that the Lord is at work in these encounters, for he promised that "where two or three are gathered together in my name, there am I in the midst of them" (Mt 18:20).

This book is built around a three-week personal retreat, but this small-group guide provides four weeks to allow one introductory gathering where you can get to know the other participants. A plan for that first meeting is included below; after that, participants should progress through the book, praying along with each day's reflections and prompts. Regather once a week to share the fruits of this process. Along the way, take note of any particularly striking or moving insights so you can bring those back to the group. The plans and discussion questions below for weeks one through three will help facilitate the sharing of these moments with one another.

Stay flexible with the conversations, and follow the movement of the Spirit. The group doesn't have to answer all the questions if one or two of them open up a fruitful line of discussion. Be attentive to the rhythms of sharing so that everyone has a chance to offer something about their experience of how the Lord moved through their prayer. Be sure to end by agreeing on a solid meeting time and place for the following week.

As you prepare to step into this gathering, take a moment to reflect on what you would like to ask of God from this experience. To fully take advantage of the group you are in, adopt an open, expectant disposition. The more you give to the group, the more fruit you will see.

# INTRODUCTORY WEEK

Welcome to the first session of this small-group experience! This is the first session of four, where we will get to know one another and set a course for the coming month. As we take this book home and pray with it each day, we'll reconvene here to discuss the ways the Lord is speaking to us and moving in our lives. This small-group gathering is intended to enhance our experience of this book, to deepen our vulnerability with the Lord, and to share our experiences with others on the same journey.

### OPENING PRAYER

Come, Holy Spirit. Lord, we give you all the honor, glory, and praise for the ways you have moved in our lives. Thank you for giving us the desire to grow closer to you, for the ways you are planning our encounter with you, and for the joy of being in your presence. Be with each of us as individuals and as a group as we open our hearts in desire for intimacy with you. Help us to be present to one another and to the Holy Spirit. Guide our conversation today and our daily prayer through the week. We ask all this in Jesus's name. Amen.

### INTRODUCTIONS

*Go around the room and have all participants introduce themselves—sharing their names, the ages of their children, and what they're looking for from the group.*

### WHAT TO EXPECT

The book is structured as a twenty-one-day personal retreat. Each of the three weeks of this retreat is built around a new theme, beginning with desire, following with encounter, and ending with joy. We will read each chapter on our own day by day, then meet up to share how the Lord moved in our prayer lives over the course of the past week. Life as a mom can be hectic, so if all you have is two minutes, use the opening prayer at the very beginning of each day. If you miss a day, don't give up. Keep going. It's fine to show up without having completed all the reading or prayer for a given week because one of the biggest benefits of this group is simple fellowship.

### DISCUSSION QUESTIONS

- What do you need from God right now?
- How do you best hear from God? What practices have helped you listen to the Lord in the past?
- Consider the three themes of this retreat: exploring our desire for God, finding ways to encounter God in our daily experiences, and discovering joy in his presence. Which of these themes feels most challenging for you right now? Why?
- Share a time in your life when you felt close to God, then describe your relationship with him today. How are these experiences alike or different?
- How are you hoping your life will change after these next few weeks?

### CLOSING PRAYER

God, your Son revealed you to us as a loving parent. We come to you with our needs, trusting in your providing care.

*Open the floor for prayer intentions.*

Lord, we place all of these intentions in your hands. Help us to stay committed to daily prayer and to respond to the ways you are moving in our lives. We ask this in Jesus's name. Amen.

### CONCLUSION

*Commit to meeting again next week. Make sure the date, time, and location are solidified before leaving.*

# WEEK 1: DESIRE

Welcome to the second session of this small group! This week we explored our desire—or lack of desire—for God. Let's pray together.

### OPENING PRAYER

Come, Holy Spirit. Thank you, Lord, for giving us the grace to desire transformation in our lives. Thank you for giving us the grace to desire to show up. Bless our conversation here today. Help us to be vulnerable and open to sharing and to receive each other well. Help us grow in desire for you through one another. We ask this in Jesus's name. Amen.

### DISCUSSION QUESTIONS

- Share with the group a general highlight from your week.
- What is something that stuck out to you from the readings or your prayer over the past seven days?
- What is a deep desire in your life right now? What do you think God is saying to you about it?
- How does desire for God manifest in your life?
- What struggles have you faced in daily prayer? What graces have you seen?
- How has your desire for God changed over the past seven days?

### CLOSING PRAYER

God, your Son revealed you to us as a loving parent. We come to you with our needs, trusting in your providing care.

*Open the floor for prayer intentions.*

Lord, we place all of these intentions in your hands. Help us to desire you and to choose you when our emotions fail us. Remind us each day that you will always satisfy us when we cry out to you. Fill us up, Lord. We ask all this in Jesus's name. Amen.

### CONCLUSION

*Commit to meeting again next week. Make sure the date, time, and location are solidified before leaving.*

## WEEK 2: ENCOUNTER

Welcome to the third gathering of this small group! This week, we explored encountering God in prayer, knowing that the Lord is near, regardless of whether we feel his presence.

### OPENING PRAYER

Come, Holy Spirit. Lord, we know you are here, present among us. Even when we don't feel you near, you are with us. Help us to stay grounded in you. Bless our conversation here today, and be present among us as we share. Make us aware of your presence, Lord, as we encounter you and one another. We ask this in Jesus's name. Amen.

### DISCUSSION QUESTIONS

- Share a general highlight from your week with the group.
- What is something that stuck out to you from the readings or your prayer over the past seven days?
- Share a time when you encountered the Lord in a significant way this week. If there was anything surprising about the experience, describe it.
- Share a time when you most needed the Lord to show up. What happened?
- How do you need the Lord to show up in your life right now?

### CLOSING PRAYER

God, your Son revealed you to us as a loving parent. We come to you with our needs, trusting in your providing care.

*Open the floor for prayer intentions.*

Lord, we place all of these intentions in your hands. Help us to recognize the ways you are inviting us to encounter you. Open our hearts to transformation and to respond when you call. Make yourself known to us, Lord. We ask this in Jesus's name. Amen.

### CONCLUSION

*Commit to meeting again next week. Make sure the date, time, and location are solidified before leaving.*

# WEEK 3: JOY

Welcome to the final session of this small group! This week we prayed with joy and looked for it apart from our earthly circumstances.

### OPENING PRAYER

Come, Holy Spirit. God, you are so good! Thank you for the love and mercy you have shown us. Thank you for the peace and joy we receive in abiding with you. Bless our discussion today. Help us to be open to you and to one another. Help us experience the joy that is totally dependent on you. We ask this in Jesus's name. Amen.

### DISCUSSION QUESTIONS

- Share a general highlight from your week with the group.
- What is something that stuck out to you from the readings or your prayer over the past seven days?
- What brings you joy? What have you allowed to steal your joy?
- In what ways can you rest in joy as distinct from earthly happiness? How might you seek joy in the midst of earthly hardship?
- Share a time you or someone you know was able to keep their joy in the midst of struggles or challenges.

### WRAP-UP CONVERSATION

*As you conclude these meetings, talk about the fruits of this experience, and establish some habits that you want to retain in the weeks ahead. These two questions might surface more wisdom from the group.*

- What has been the most helpful part of this small group for you?
- What is a practice you intend to use to keep up a habit of daily prayer?

### CLOSING PRAYER

God, your Son revealed you to us as a loving parent. We come to you with our needs, trusting in your providing care.

*Open the floor for prayer intentions.*

Lord, we place all of these intentions in your hands. Give us joy that rests in you alone. Help us not to be dependent on our outward circumstances. Instead help us to be dependent on you and to look for the joy that only you can give. Help us to be vigilant when our joy is in danger of being stolen. Help us to choose joy in every circumstance. We ask this in Jesus's name. Amen.

**JENNIFER STAVINOHA** is a ministry leader, writer, and content creator for Ablaze Ministries. She has developed online courses and videos for Ablaze Families, presents for the Catholic Foundations Series by Forte Catholic, and serves as the theological editor for the *Every Sacred Sunday Mass* journals. She speaks regularly at parishes, schools, and retreats.

Stavinoha earned a bachelor's degree in religious studies from the University of Incarnate Word and a master's degree in theology and Christian ministry from Franciscan University of Steubenville.

Stavinoha lives in Bryan, Texas, with her husband and children.

Website: jenstavinoha.com
Facebook: @AblazeFamilies
Instagram: @ablazefamilies
YouTube: @AblazeFamilies

**ALLISON SULLIVAN** is host of the *Sinner Saint Sister* podcast and author of *Rock Paper Scissors: God's Mighty Power, Jesus' Covering Forgiveness, and the Snipping Refinement of the Holy Spirit.*

AVE

Ave Maria Press

Founded in 1865, Ave Maria Press, a ministry of the Congregation of Holy Cross, is a Catholic publishing company that serves the spiritual and formative needs of the Church and its schools, institutions, and ministers; Christian individuals and families; and others seeking spiritual nourishment.

For a complete listing of titles from

Ave Maria Press

Sorin Books

Forest of Peace

Christian Classics

visit www.avemariapress.com

AVE | Ave Maria Press
Notre Dame, IN

A Ministry of the United States Province of Holy Cross